LETTERS

WRITTEN DURING A TRIP

TO

SOUTHERN INDIA & CEYLON

IN THE

WINTER OF 1876-1877

LETTERS

WRITTEN DURING A TRIP

TO

SOUTHERN INDIA & CEYLON

IN THE

WINTER OF 1876-1877

C. R. WILLIAMS

GYAN

Published by

Gyan Publishing House
5, Ansari Road
Daryaganj, New Delhi-110002
Phone: 011-47034999, 9811692060
E-mail: books@gyanbooks.com

Distribution Network
gyanbooks.com
India, USA, Canada, UK, Australia

ISBN: 978-93-7133-723-6 (PB)

First Published, 1877

2nd Impression 2025

Printed at: Gyan Press, Delhi.

LETTERS WRITTEN DURING A TRIP TO SOUTHERN INDIA & CEYLON: IN THE WINTER OF 1876-1877

Author: C. R. WILLIAMS

LETTERS

WRITTEN DURING A TRIP

TO

SOUTHERN INDIA & CEYLON

IN THE

WINTER OF 1876—1877.

With Original Illustrations.

(PRINTED FOR PRIVATE CIRCULATION.)

London:
PRINTED BY C. ROWORTH & SONS,
NEWTON STREET, HIGH HOLBORN.

1877.

PREFACE.

In the autumn of last year it was proposed to me to accompany my brother, the Boden Professor of Sanskrit at Oxford, on his intended tour in Southern India; the objects he had in view in undertaking the journey being connected with his chair. After thirty-five years and upwards passed in the daily routine of professional life in London, I was glad of such a novel and interesting break. I accepted the proposal, and accompanied him. The following Letters were written as I travelled through the country. They are descriptive of my personal experiences only, and have been collected and are now printed for private circulation, in order to convey to my family and immediate friends the same pleasure which I myself enjoy in looking on rapid sketches from Nature done on the spot and not touched afterwards. The outline of our tour was as follows. We took our passage from Southampton, *viâ* the Suez Canal, direct to Bombay. Thence by rail due north to Ahmedabad, in Guzerat, about 300 miles distant from Bombay, and back to Bombay. Thence a fresh start by rail to Madras, stopping at Poona, and visiting the Sanitarium of Mahabaleshwur. From Madras to Ootacamund and the Nielgherries, and from thence southwards to Tanjore, Trichinopoly, and Madura. From Madura by country roads to the Island of Paumben, and thence by sea to Tuticorin. The rail took us from Tuticorin inland to Palamcottah and Tinnevelly and back to the coast again, and we embarked thence for Ceylon. From Ceylon my brother retraced his steps by rail to Madras, having further information to obtain there. I took the coasting vessel along the Malabar coast to Bombay. We met in Bombay; and, after a visit to the temples of Ellora, returned together to England *viâ* Brindisi and Venice, stopping a week in Cairo *en route*. The illustrations are my own.

C. R. WILLIAMS.

62, Lincoln's Inn Fields,
May, 1877.

SS. "NEPAUL,"
Sunday, 15th October, 1876.

IT is time I should begin a letter to you, but although it is time I could not have commenced sooner, for the Bay of Biscay completely polished me off, and I only was able to crawl out of my berth during the afternoon of yesterday for the first time. We had a fair run down the Channel, passing the fortifications on both sides of the Solent, which I had never seen before, and the Lighthouse at the extremity of the Needles; then, dinner over, at which I was as sprightly as possible, admiring the saloon of the ship brilliantly lighted along its whole length of upwards of 100 feet, the lights reflected by mirrors, and more like a Parisian first-class café than a thing on the ocean, I turned in. The next morning, resolved to begin my new life as I intended to continue it, I got up at six, and, after pursuing a very devious path to the baths amidships, contrived to have a sea-water bath. But I soon found that we were in the Chops of the Channel—a very different matter from the Solent—and when I got back to my berth I felt quite disabled. There I remained all Friday, all Friday night, and until 2 o'clock yesterday, dreadfully ill. I had no idea that I was such a bad sailor, but then I had never before been so tried. Poor Stanley was worse than myself—not so Monier, who was nothing more than squeamish, and instead of our looking after him he was our friend and nurse, and gave us his advice and assistance on his legs as if he were the ship doctor. We passed Ushant (not visible) about 10 on Friday morning, and then fairly entered the Bay of Biscay. Most provoking, the weather was fine and even sunny overhead and no wind, but we had arrived at the tail of three weeks of unexceptionably stormy weather coming from the south-west. The "Mongolia" and the "Pekin," the two ships which had preceded us a week and a fortnight previously, had made bad passages. The "Pekin" had had some of her boats carried away, and shipped a sea at one time of fifty tons, doing a deal of damage. We had no such storms, but we came in for the Atlantic rollers—huge hills of sea, unbroken in surface, careering after each other at intervals of 200 or 300 yards from west to east, whereas our course was from north to south, so these great hills caught us broadside on, causing the ship to roll in a most uncomfortable manner; and this continued for thirty-six hours, until we had passed Cape Finisterre yesterday afternoon. I had incautiously left the scuttle open just over my berth to get fresh air; the ship rolled her lee side right under this scuttle, and in came the sea at the rate of a dozen fireplugs, drenching my bed and myself as if we had all been soused in the Bay. Ill as I was, I scrambled up, screwed in the bull's-eye, threw off my bedding, and did my best to change my things, and then lay down again in the most damp and miserable condition. Often and often did I ask myself, "Oh, Dolly, why did I leave your lovely valley and luxurious life for such misery as this?" But all is over, and Richard's himself again. We expect to reach Gibraltar late to-morrow night or early Tuesday morning, and so I am writing now in preparation. The vessel is a fine one—3,600 tons—iron—new this year—600 horse-power—355 feet long—40 feet beam—flush deck from end to end, which gives it an appearance of great length. The crew is composed of seven English quarter-masters and forty-three Lascar seamen, six English engineers, thirty firemen (Mussulmans), and fifteen Sidi men or negroes

Sidi Boy
playing on the one stringed Banjo
Nepaul.
Sunday 22 Oct.

for coal shifters. It really is extraordinary that the responsible government of this huge and complicated ship should practically be in the hands of thirteen Englishmen only, independently of the officers. The Lascar seamen are puny creatures, dressed in fancy dresses, but all with picturesque turbans, naked feet, and apparently unfit for any physical exertion. The Sidi men are scarcely human—negroes from Mozambique of the coarsest kind—very different type from the Lascars—big, muscular men, semi-nude, some without hair, others with ridges of wool along the head and chin like the furrows of a ploughed field. I would have given a good deal for a photograph of a batch of these fellows, sitting in limp attitudes on the iron grating over the boiler room before we started, grinning and chattering like huge baboons, very soon to descend 35 feet to the very bottom of the ship to keep up the fires below. It is a pandemonium into which, looking down the grating, we see these creatures working in the bright glare of the furnaces at a depth where no air can reach them; yet, when airing themselves on the grating, they appear in tip-top spirits and as happy as kings. Gladstone or Disraeli might give a good deal to exchange with a Sidi man, if happiness be the sole object of life. 12 o'clock. We have just finished Divine service in the saloon—the captain reading from a cushion covered with the Union Jack. The Lascars have swarmed up the rigging, notwithstanding their naked feet, and have set all the square sails of the ship, and she is bowling along with a rattling breeze aft, a heavy but beautiful sea surging from her bows—such a sea as Melby delights to paint, like molten lead, with touches of colour here and there rivalling the flashes of the finest gems. I am seated on the planks of the live-stock boxes, high above the gunwale, writing this, and every now and then looking off to enjoy the magnificent prospect of sea and sky. From this you will know that I have recovered from the effects of the

Bay and am delighting in the scene. Live-stock boxes remind me to tell you that we have a large number of live sheep on board, coops on coops of ducks and poultry, and a few turkeys and geese; a cow with her calf, poor things; the calf is tied to the head of the box so as to induce the cow to give her milk, but not to the calf. Poor cow, so soft and sleepy-eyed, in a small wooden box, such a different field to that which is her due. Old Mair would declare that he never saw "sich a byre" in all his life. We have also a horse, several dogs, and a monkey. Our passengers number about 150 first-class and 30 second. There are amongst them Lady Napier of Magdala, Colonel Mostyn of the 23rd Fusiliers, Captain Curzon and several civilians, some of whom are known to Monier. A good many we shall drop at Gibraltar, and then the crowd will be diminished. At present we have two breakfasts, one at 8.30, the other at 9; and two dinners, one at 5, the other at 6. To attend to these, there is a capital caboose and staff of cooks. Here again, the chief only is English, the others natives, with twenty stewards and waiters, a mixed lot of English, Portuguese, Maltese, &c. The dinners are excellent—soup and fish, two entrées, two joints, always curry, the condiments being ground daily for it, sweets and dessert. All this is found by the company for the passage-money—wines and liquors extra. There is also the purser or head purveyor—an intelligent man—with whom only, amongst the officers, I have had any talk. He says that this is a fair average passage; only twice in his experience of fifty voyages has he had it smooth: once he was caught in the P. & O. SS. "Zambesi" in a gale off Cape Finisterre—she went through it, but the "La Plata" of the same size turned tail to run before the wind, and a huge sea fell on her poop and literally crushed her down to the bottom. Two other large steamers foundered in the same gale. I can quite imagine it from the enormous size and violence and velocity of the waves I have myself now witnessed. I forgot,—we have also on board the Thakore of Limrie, a chief of Kattywar, but he has not been seen since he appeared on deck in gorgeous apparel at Southampton.

My fear now is that we shall arrive at Gibraltar about midnight to-morrow, and so lose the sight of it, and, perhaps, the opportunity of landing. You will know, however, from receiving this that we *have* arrived, and that the most disagreeable part of our voyage is over.

I have given you an egotistical story here, but it will be acceptable to you. I do not change my affections with the sky—they are still at home and as warm as ever.

Monday morning, 16th Oct. I am yet able to add to my letter. The climate improves every day, and I am writing in my usual place on deck under a brilliant sky, a warm sun, and the (now) indigo sea sparkling beneath me. All the rolling swell has ceased, and the ship is passing rapidly through the water with scarcely any motion. Stanley appeared in public life for the first time this morning at breakfast, and I hope will now hold his own. For myself I have forgotten the anguish of the Bay, and am in high health, appetite and spirits. One needs an appetite for the sake of the living on board. Our breakfast this morning was haddock, rumpsteak and onions, sausages, savoury omelette, curry, and various collaterals. At 1 we have tiffin of various dishes, and at 5 dinner. How the cooks manage it would puzzle even Pickett, good cook as she is—tell her I remember her here off the coast of Portugal—but certain it is that these meals, *two* breakfasts and *two* dinners, mind, are served up each day to 150 people hot and well dressed from a kitchen not so large as ours in Green Street.

We sighted land for the first time yesterday afternoon

about 5. It was the high land at the entrance to the Tagus; then night closed on us, and this morning we awoke to a brilliant sunrise lighting up the splendid cliffs of Cape St. Vincent. It was a glorious sight. We ran close to these grand perpendicular walls of rock, of a rich burnt sienna colour, crowned with lighthouses at intervals, and all radiant in the morning sun. Now we are running straight for Gibraltar, which I fear will be reached after dark to-night, and so we shall be cramped for time to land and see what we ought to see there. But the sight of the Rock from the ship will almost suffice for me. We must all come out to Gibraltar for the winter if we can manage it. You shall hear from me again from Malta.

SS. "NEPAUL," MEDITERRANEAN,
Wednesday, 18*th October*, 1876.

THIS, my second letter to you, is commenced whilst we are running before a prosperous wind, but with a sea and sky as murky as any our English coast can boast, and it is raining heavily, varied by thunder and lightning. Not Mediterranean weather certainly, and very different to what Monier experienced last October. The temperature is cool as a consequence; according to Adelaide's thermometer, now hanging up in our cabin, 65°. But let me hasten to Gibraltar. We arrived there at 2 o'clock yesterday morning, of course quite dark. I could not rest in bed, and so soon as the screw stopped I slipped on an overcoat over my nightgown and ran up the steps of the forehatch to see what I could see. Nothing definite, only the dim outline of Algesiras Bay and of the Rock and the lights of the town reflected in the water; all pretty, but it might have been Wapping or Dover, so I turned into bed again and remained there till dawn. At 6 I dressed and went on deck again and saw more clearly the outline of the celebrated Rock rising abruptly at the back of the town (not the best point of view of the Rock) and of Ape's Hill, corresponding with the rock on the other side of the Straits, the two being the two pillars of Hercules. Whilst endeavouring to make out the landscape I observed a Levanter, or one of the sharp Mediterranean squalls, coming on, and in a moment the gust came down and the bay was broken up into foam. Colonel Mostyn told me that they had had no rain at Gibraltar for eight or nine months, and that it was expected and anxiously. October was the month for it. So here it came as we came, and a great bore for us.

However the squall ceased, and directly afterwards I heard a gentleman on board inquiring for us, and it proved to be a clerk from Mr. Cuby, a resident merchant in Gibraltar, to whom Frank Hallett had written to announce us. He had got a boat alongside, which he and our three selves got into, and we landed at the pier, where Mr. Cuby himself met us. He had a carriage and guide waiting for us on the pier, so no time was lost, and never was time more valuable, for we landed at 6.30, and the "Nepaul" was to start for Malta at 9. We drove through the streets of the narrow town, occupying a narrow flat slip of land at the base of the Rock, up to the entrance to the gallery commanding the Spanish frontier. Along this gallery we were conducted by an artilleryman, and from two successive platforms on to which the gallery debouched we had a glorious view over the neutral ground or neck of land which makes the Rock a peninsula bounded by the Bay of Algesiras on one side and the Mediterranean on the other, with the Spanish mountains beyond.

We rejoined the carriage on the flat and drove to the neutral ground, from which, looking back, we had a view of the Rock, and then to the market place in the town, through which we walked, and an exciting scene it was, as indeed, though in a modified degree, was the whole of the town. Spaniards pouring into the market on huge mules gaily caparisoned; mules with flag-basket panniers full of produce, some carrying casks of wine; mules which had delivered their burthen, tethered in long rows along the streets; Spaniards in the orthodox costume of their country, black squat hats, gay sashes; Moors got up in turbans, tunics and slippers; Jews and Rabbis in long robes and peculiar head gear; all mixed up with our own soldiery in various uniforms. Then there were brilliant tomatoes, brinjalls, figs, grapes, gourds and melons, and other produce in keeping. Flocks of goats ready to be milked, horses, country carts, all jostling each other, and forming an exciting scene for a man just landed from Green Street, Grosvenor Square. I will not dilate on the Rock itself—it is one of the wonders of the world. In colour it was brown, for the long dry weather had burnt it up. The foliage at the base, too, consisting of fig trees with trunks as big as my body, date, palm, castor oil tree, pepper tree, cactus, prickly pear, was dried up. But in spring, as the face of the Rock is covered with tufts of vegetation, the colours must be very varied and lovely. Then we drove back through the town to the Alameida, or pleasure garden, and finally at 9 to the pier, where we found Mr. Cuby again, waiting to say farewell. He would not hear of our paying. "All is paid for," he said, and then we pulled back in the same boat to the "Nepaul." Just as we re-embarked the rain commenced again, and we weighed anchor in wind and rain, getting our last view of the Rock as we rounded Europa Point, as Turner might have wished to paint it, veiled in mist and mystery. The same weather has followed us, and we caught but a cloudy outline of the Sierra Nevada on the Spanish coast yesterday, and a similar glimpse of the mountains on the African coast to-day. As I write, it has been raining for four hours, and no sign of ceasing as yet. There is a sea on, but not making much impression on this large vessel. I think these two sights, Cape St. Vincent as we saw it in the morning sun, and Gibraltar, will remain with me to my dying day. What is in store for me remains to be proved, but those two are enough for the greediest traveller. At Gibraltar we parted with Colonel Mostyn, Captain Curzon and Mr. Verner, the former commanding the 23rd (Colonel Bunbury's old regiment), the two latter in the Rifle Brigade. With all these we made friends. Verner is a capital artist, and produced his book of caricatures, over which we had some merriment. Colonel Mostyn is a son of the old lord of our county, and we consequently had some subjects in common. It is surprising how soon one gets to look 'on a ship as one's home. I now know every turn and corner of the "Nepaul," and find our cabin as comfortable as any state room on terra firma; more especially as our Gibraltar friends leaving us has enabled the captain to give us separate cabins. Noises which at Dolly would awaken the dead are here almost necessary to sleep. The ship is worked by steam, sails hoisted, anchors and heavy things moved by means of a steam winch, not by manual labour. This thing works often at night with a crash and clatter which at Dolly would be audible at Llanelltyd. I seldom hear it. Then we have the racket and singing of sailors, cackling of hens, barking of dogs, scrubbing of decks, quarterly bells, bumpings and thumpings from causes unknown, but they are as nothing. One noise we in the fore part of the ship escape, and that is the grind and motion of the screw; not that that would be any grievance. On the other hand there are many comforts,—the sea-bath in the morning. I slip on my dressing-gown at six every morning and hurry to one of the half-dozen marble baths in the ship, turn on a huge brass cock, and out rushes a volume of sea-water fit to knock you down, often sparkling with phosphorescence. There is a black attendant on the baths, and one also on the w.c.'s, which latter are admirably contrived and conducted. We have plenty of clean towels and fresh water, soap, &c., &c., and our bed-room steward is in and out constantly to clean up and make tidy and to minister to our wants in every way. Our pleasantest passengers are Colonel Chamier, one of the Deputy Commissioners of Oude, Captain and Mrs. Greig and his sister—he was formerly in the 92nd regiment, but is now attached to the Forest Department in the North-Western Provinces,—Mr. Bernard, one of the Commissioners of the Central Provinces, Mr. Willock (a son of old Sir

Henry), also in the Civil Service and high up, and two or three pleasant young officers and civilians.

Thursday, 19th Oct. Awoke about midnight by the hoarse sound of the fog-horn, a noise which, as distinguished from the others, struck on my nerves as the note of alarm, and woke me up immediately. I looked out of the port-hole and found the rain descending in torrents and the weather dark and thick, engines slowed and occasionally stopping altogether. A strange sensation is that of an unseen and unintelligible danger in a dark night on the sea. This continued for an hour, but proceeded from nothing except the caution of the captain. This morning the weather has taken up, and we are running before a grand breeze, directly aft, with all our square sails set,—the sea being much more of the deep sapphire colour peculiar to the Mediterranean, the big waves crested with white foam; the dim outline of the African coast visible, as were the lights of Algiers as we passed that place about 7 o'clock yesterday evening,—thermometer in our cabin 70°. The day is one to be remembered from the extreme beauty of the sea and sky. No words can describe the colour of the sea, crisped and frothed up by the fresh breeze, so that the top of every sapphire wave had its flash of emerald or chrysolite. We hope to make Malta by midnight to-morrow, where this will be posted.

Friday, 20th Oct. We have experienced every variety of Mediterranean weather except a calm. This morning we have a brisk breeze on our beam and are bowling along with all sails set fore and aft; the sea is in considerable commotion, sufficient to disable several of our passengers,—not myself, fortunately. The pace of the ship is too good for us, for we shall arrive at Malta about 7 o'clock this evening, coal in the night, and be off early, I fear, on Saturday morning. The captain advises us to go to the opera, built, if I remember right, by Edward Barry, and that we must do, but I should have preferred daylight and the streets of the town. This morning at 8 we passed the Island of Pantalaria, the scene of Shakespeare's Tempest—at least, there is no one to contradict the assertion—a volcanic island rising from both sides of the sea into a double cone, of a lovely violet colour as we saw it. Our next land will be Malta. There is a young officer on board, a Captain Maurice of the 101st Regiment, now quartered at Malta. I have given him my card, and he has promised to call when next in England. I hope, also, to keep several others on board as friends hereafter. We saw several small shoals of flying fish during our run yesterday trying to escape from the ship; they spring out of the water like silver swallows, skim along the surface for a considerable distance, I should say 150 or 200 yards, and then splash down again—not so large as I expected them to be, but brighter and more silvery. Every one is pleased with the ship, which is seaworthy and fast and clean, and sweet inside, and the captain has our confidence, partly because he is not too sociable or communicative.

SS. "Nepaul,"
Saturday, 21st October, 1876.

I like to write to you whilst scenes are fresh in my memory, and for that reason I commence my letter within three hours after leaving Malta, although there is no prospect of my being able to post it until we reach Suez, and that will not be for four or five days yet. You are always in my thoughts, and the great resource of my sea-going life is to hold converse with you in this way. We arrived at Malta at 9 o'clock last night, after an unusually quick run from Gibraltar, attended, however, with a good deal of sea at times. Although we were off the mouth of the harbour at 9, we were more than an hour getting in. The night was dark, the entrance small, and our vessel long, and the captain missed his shot the first time, and we were nearly on the rocks, but he backed astern full speed and we made a retreat and gyration, and eventually steamed in and anchored in the quarantine harbour. It was too late to land—some did—but we thought it prudent to get some sleep and begin early this morning. The captain had alarmed us by saying that he intended to coal as fast as he could and be off by 6 o'clock this morning. But I remonstrated with him against such unnecessary haste and entreated him to give us tourists an opportunity of seeing the place. Whether from courtesy or from necessity the notice was issued at night that the ship would not sail till 12 o'clock to-day. The captain is not to be blamed for over-anxiety, for their mail contract obliges them to be at Suez waiting there for the Brindisi mail, and the transit through the Canal is always one of great uncertainty, getting stuck oneself or following some other vessel who has stuck immediately before you, and so they like to take time by the forelock. We remained on board therefore, and were amused at night by watching the crowd of shore boats cluster round the ship, in shape like gondolas, with high prows and sterns, each one carrying a lantern which lit up the forms of the swarthy Maltese boatmen and caused all sorts of pretty effects in the dark water. We were, moreover, close to the land, and the scene at night was very striking. We dressed at 6 this morning, and were disappointed to meet with rain and heavy sky. The temperature was sultry in the extreme, betokening storm. Nevertheless, we landed at once, selected a guide from the swarms who pounced down on us, and walked successively to the Church of St. John, the only peculiar feature of which was the mosaic pavement made of marbles of varied colours and precious stones, recording the names, arms and military feats of the knights of the Order. Then to the armoury, opera house, &c., afterwards taking a carriage to the gardens of St. Antonio, four miles off, which enabled us to see something of the country. The whole island is a volcanic rock, with scarcely any vegetation—except in the gardens of St. Antonio there is not a tree worthy of the name. The whole place is identical with the photographs and drawings I have seen of Jerusalem or Damascus—a dry, burnt-up tufa soil, walls of the same based on the natural rock, the prevailing colour being yellow; the houses built of the same rock, yellow also, and all flat-roofed. All round are the frowning fortifications which guard the two harbours, and form a hard framework to a dry rectangular burnt-up picture. The streets, however, when once inside them, are picturesque. Except the two main streets, they are orientally narrow and steep, with many picturesque projections in the shape of balconies, oriel windows, &c. The population is more Italian than Spanish, the vehicles, both by sea and land, being decidedly Italian. We had rain throughout our tour, but no storm, and after we had done the place we were done ourselves in the attempt to shop and buy a few mementoes of the visit. Lace, coral and sponges seem to be the staple of the island, and the sellers of them are Jews, the most exacting of their race. I went into a shop and asked the price of some lace. "This veil," the rascal replied, "is 30*s*. Observe the work (placing it against some white paper); not like the rubbish the fellows sell on board the steamboat,—finest Maltese work, observe the Maltese cross," &c., &c. "Very good," I said, and then taking up three collars and cuffs, and two lengths of lace for trimming, and two other veils, I put them altogether with the original veil and said, "now I'll give you 15*s*. for the lot." Such an outcry proceeded from the rascal, but I stood to my guns. My next move was to take up my hat and walk out of the shop. He doubled round the counter in no time, and pulled me back. £5, he said, was the cost price of the lot, but he would take £4 : 10*s*. "Nonsense," I said, "I'll give you 17*s*. 6*d*." It ended in my getting the whole for a pound; and I believe he did me after all. This very same fellow afterwards appeared on the deck of our ship, before we sailed, with his pack of goods, and was hard at work, with a host of his co-vendors, dealing with the passengers, all of them invariably beginning with £8 or £10, and handing over the article eventually for £1 or £1 : 10*s*. And after all the lace has a suspicious Nottingham look about it.

We returned to our vessel by 12 o'clock, and here we are on our way and out of sight of land, steaming to Port Said. The temperature of Malta was that of a hothouse, and I was running down with moisture. Thermometer in our cabin on our return 80°. This accounts for the oleander in full flower, orange trees in great profusion and full of fruit, pepper tree, palm, prickly pear, &c., all of which are indigenous in the island.

Sunday. A dreadful sirocco has been blowing all last night and all to-day; the heat at 80°, and yet a cold wind. Several passengers are laid up with it, added to which we have had a cloudy sky and rolling sea. There has been bad weather all about us, and the sea is up in consequence. We had a decent service in the morning with a good choir, previous to which the ship's crew mustered on deck, the quartermasters and Lascars in file on one side, the firemen and stokers on the other, the negroes turning out in long snow-white gowns, headed by their chiefs, who wore gold-braided jackets, so different from their work-day attire. They looked so strange, the two long rows of blacks dressed so picturesquely, the Lascars in blue with red turbans, the negroes in white and scull caps of fancy cut and colours. Did you observe how appropriate the Psalm of the day was to my condition at this moment? We cannot, however, think of each other doing the same thing at the same time. My London watch makes it 7 p.m., whereas our time here is 8.30, an hour and a-half's difference.

Monday. Fickle Mediterranean! the sirocco has gone, the sea has subsided, the temperature fallen, and we are rejoicing in blue sky and a sea of ultramarine. The first really calm sea we have had since we left England. The ladies have put on their finery, the gentlemen clean shirts, and the deck has assumed the aspect of Kensington Gardens on a summer afternoon. Thermometer at 2 p.m. in our cabin 76°. To-day you are at Wokingham. How different our relative surroundings! Every stage brings more and more novelty to me. On Wednesday we shall be in the Canal, and actually in the East. Our foretaste of the East to-day has been the rigging out of punkahs in the saloon—they are four in number, all in a line along the whole length of the saloon, and are pulled by four black boys stationed at regular intervals at the side of the saloon, all four dressed alike, in long white shirts, red sashes and red turbans—the beau ideal of the black boy I have always wished for as a little slave of my own. We have also to-day put up the *double* awning on deck, one above the other, leaving a space of about a foot between the two.

Tuesday night. Another heavenly day, preceded by a dawn of the most exquisite fantastic colours. Pen cannot describe the colours. Sea smooth as glass, and a fresh balmy breeze tempering all. The ship has to-day had the appearance of a pleasure party out for the day on the Lake of Geneva. No incident, however, to recount, and therefore I will give you the day. Up at 6.30 and donned my dressing-gown and slippers, and, sponge and towels in hand, hastened to one of the marble baths in the ship. I say hastened, because the baths are the prize of a competitive scramble, and it is first come first served. Before I left the cabin, however, I stuck my head out of the port-hole and there was enchanted for a few moments by the dawn I have referred to. Hurrah, found a bath vacant, got into it in a twinkling, and turned on the great brass cock right on to my back, sponged and rolled about, the strong briny water making my eyes smart again. Towelled myself and had a fresh-water rinse in a tub, always placed in the bath-room on purpose. Back into my cabin, and dressed and up on deck and chatted with Colonel Chamier for an hour before breakfast, to which I descended at 8.30—a hot breakfast, with *menu* of a series of dishes, and always ending with curry. Then on deck reclining in my own easy chair, with my sketching materials about me jotting down any figure which might attract my notice, the double awning sheltering me from a glorious sun, the sea glassy and lovely in colour, and breeze fresh and soft. Lunch at one. Then on deck again, and again in my easy chair, chatting and reading till five; when dinner, several courses of well-cooked food, being served up, the punkahs going all the time. By the time dinner was ended the moon had risen, and I have been walking the deck with the moon on the sea till now, 8 p.m., when I have again dived down into the saloon, punkahs still going, poor little black boys, to write this to you. We are fifty miles from Port Said, which we hope to reach by midnight, and to enter the Canal at break of day to-morrow. I shall be up by sunrise to-morrow morning to witness our entrance into the Canal, and shall be on deck all day to watch our progress through it; therefore my description of the Canal must be kept for my Aden letter.

Wednesday, 25th Oct. Actually in the East at last. We made Port Said at 6.30 this morning, and entered the Canal soon afterwards. What a new world it is! Men, costume, houses, country, climate, all eastern as if by the touch of a wand. We are now slowly passing through the Canal, the banks enlivened by camels now and then, and groups of Egyptians engaged in facing or otherwise repairing the Canal. Dense masses of flamingoes and pelicans crowd the lagoons on either side, and animal life shows itself also in the house flies, which have begun to torment us as they did Pharaoh of old. We arrive at Suez to-morrow about noon—if we don't stick in the Canal.

Thursday, 26th Oct., 1 o'clock. Just arrived at Suez. But we are told that we must post our letters at once, without waiting to acknowledge our home letters. I am sorry for this, but will write, of course, from Aden.

Approach to Suez from the Canal 26 Oct. 1876

p. 18.

p. 18.

SS. "Nepaul," Gulf of Suez,
Friday, 27*th October*, 1876.

How refreshing were your letters received at 2 o'clock this afternoon, just before we cast off our moorings at Suez and started for Aden! I ran over the bundles of letters brought on board by the P. & O. agent for our passengers, seized Ro's first; the agent said, "That's all for you, sir;" "I swear there's another," I replied, "I know it, I'll swear it." At last, in another bundle, I found yours, and took both up with me on deck to devour at leisure. It did seem so strange, looking down from the deck on the quay, which was alive with Egyptians, Arabs, Nubians, negroes, in every variety of turban and costume, with the burning range of arid mountains bounding the plain of Suez immediately facing me, the ship taking in the mails, bullion, cargo, and I in my cane chair in the corner of the deck, and yet as if by magic transported to Dolly, the neighbours, old Mair, the mare and foal, Craven Cottage, the new cob, &c. However, the result on my mind was that of inexpressible relief and comfort, and I placed the letters in my pocket and walked the deck a new man, why I cannot explain, but so much has occurred to me since we parted that I could not help fancying you had much and of a varied kind to communicate also. Now, I am satisfied till we reach Bombay, when we shall get more letters. We arrived at Suez (as I told you in a hurried postscript to the letter which I posted to you yesterday) at 1 o'clock yesterday. The vessel was moored alongside the quay, and after lunch I prevailed on Monier to give up the transit to Suez, three miles off, by boat, and take donkeys instead. These animals and their Arab or Nubian owners are clustered a short distance from the ship, and, as soon as a likely customer is seen approaching, each owner with his particular donkey rushes at him, circles round him, shouts at him, "Good donkey, sare;" "This Dr. Kenealy, sare;" "This Dr. Gully, sare;" "Me show you everyting, sare;" and so on. We three got separated in the scrimmage. I can generally take care of myself, selected my animal with a practised eye, shoved off the crowd, mounted my animal at once, and flourished my white-covered umbrella in triumph. Monier was not so fortunate, and when we met at Suez he told me he had been tied to a wrong donkey with a strap, from which the owners of five other donkeys, all of whom claimed him, struggled in vain to release him. The strap fellow had got Monier as tight as a whistle, and there he and the donkey, both tied together, were revolving on a double axis, the five other donkeys and their owners revolving round him again like a kind of solar system, all shouting and struggling as if just released from Bedlam. How Monier eventually disengaged himself from the strap and the wrong donkey he himself does not know, but I waited for him at Suez till he came up all red hot and dishevelled, his helmet awry and his ever-present plaid dragging behind him. He inquired why Stanley did not come to the rescue, but Stanley had his conflict also; and, not versed in equitation, he had as much as he could do to get on, and afterwards to hold on by the large round smooth pummel which is common to all Suez saddles, and then his donkey being evidently some relation of mine came after me at a hand canter, quite irrespective of the wishes and dutiful notions of his rider. The scene presented to me a very comic phase, as gravely narrated to me by the learned professor. Well, but Suez is a sight when you enter it: the narrow irregular streets called the bazaar, the open dens called shops, in which, or on the goods themselves, are seated the sellers, cross-legged or reclining, the mattings and awnings overhead, the varied crowd of Bedouin Arabs,

Nubians, Moors, negroes, Egyptians, blind beggars, women with covered faces, water carriers, donkeys, singing strollers; and such costumes, without exaggeration I may say every one different, and every one a study for a painter. Then in the open spaces of the town, cafés with sultans, grand viziers and Othellos (apparently) reclining on rattan benches smoking their hookahs, camels, goats and sheep of a very different breed from our sheep, with their extraordinary owners, wearing perhaps the identical clothing which Abraham wore when he was in these parts, and which had never been washed since. It was a wonderful introduction for me to eastern life in its most characteristic, and, I should add, dirtiest form; the dirt of the wretched streets and the smell were simply overpowering, and, excited as I was by the wonderful scene, I stuck my handkerchief to my nose after a couple of hours of gazing and lionizing, and was forced to exclaim, "I have had enough of this, let us seek our donkeys and return to the ship;" and we did so accordingly, the return being comparatively harmonious, our dear little donkeys ambling and cantering along, neck and neck, charmingly, the Arab boys running behind. On looking back, a dangerous experiment, as the stirrups are on a loose strap merely thrown over the back of the animal, and if you lean on one stirrup down it goes and up goes the other,—I say on looking back it was amusing to see these three black imps with long blue gowns and red fezzes tearing after us, each holding our white-covered umbrellas over his head and making the most of his opportunities—we had given them our umbrellas to carry. The Brindisi mail did not arrive till 12.30 to-day, and brought with it, unfortunately, an accession of forty-nine passengers, so that we now have an overcrowded ship.

Saturday, 28th Oct. We are out of the Gulf of Suez and are fairly in the Red Sea, the rugged outline of the hot and sterile range of mountains on the west coast being distinctly visible. We passed the Sinaitic range on the other side during the night. The sea is ultramarine blue again, but the temperature decidedly warm, 85° last night when I went to bed in our cabin, and 81° this morning at 6 when I went to the bath, the water of the bath quite tepid in consequence. I am quite well, however, and enjoying the voyage. Monier is engaged writing a short account of the Suez Canal to send to the "Times." There is much to say about it. It is certainly a noble monument to the skill and indomitable energy of one man, viz., Lesseps, and the world has become awakened to it at last. In itself, it is merely a Canal 120 feet wide, except where it debouches at intervals into the two Bitter Lakes, one of which is of great extent, and both have been converted, by the letting in of the two seas, from swampy marshes into large expanses of water, so large as from the natural operations of evaporation and condensation to cause clouds, and influence the atmosphere of the locality. The Canal will need a deal of work to protect the banks and keep it open. The wash of the steamers (we know what the wash of a penny boat is on the Thames) is simply destruction to the sandy banks, which must be pitched in with solid masonry along its whole length. Groups of Egyptians and Nubians are already employed at intervals on the banks repairing after a fashion, and these form picturesque groups as seen from the deck of the ship—the desert also beyond, with herds of loose camels browsing on the scrub, or an occasional heavily-laden camel with its owner passing along, form objects of appropriate interest. All very well for the tourist, but as a permanent means of transit, reconstruction is inevitable, and the sooner we English take it into our own hands and clap our own navvies on it the better. The length of the Canal is 100 miles, and we were about 17 hours going through it, not counting our stoppage for the night. The quay at Suez, docks, and causeway, thence to the town, are great works, and appear to have been well and solidly done. At Suez yesterday, I received a kind letter from L. Fletcher, inviting me to stay with him at Bombay, but I shall decline, as it is necessary we three should keep together, our future plans being quite in the clouds, and dependent on what we can learn about Kattywar, and the means of transit thence, through Rajpootana to Ajmeer, on our arrival at Bombay. Amongst the Brindisi passengers, I have made friends accidentally with Mr. Molesworth, the Consulting Engineer to Government for the Indian Railways, and who succeeded Major Skinner as Director of Public Works at Ceylon. Skinner's name acted like a talisman, and we were friends in a moment. There are a good many pleasant men on board, but too great a crowd. What horrid photographs those perpetrated at Dolly! Still it is something here, on the Red Sea, to look on them, unflattering as they are. I prefer home and domestic news to European politics. Russia and Turkey are all very well in their way when I am seated by the fireside in Green Street, but when I am 4,000 miles from home, give me home news to think about. Nevertheless, it would be awkward if, on our return voyage, we were captured by a Russian frigate and sent off to Siberia. This has been a Red Sea day—the temperature 85° in the port or cool cabins—much hotter on the starboard side—a lovely after-glow at sunset with a brilliant moon, nearly at the full, and a magnificent canopy of stars overhead. Sea smooth. The tide of life on board the ship is at its busiest. I pity the stewards. They are up at 5 in the morning scrubbing the lower decks and avenues to the cabins, cleaning boots and shoes, and preparing tea for the sleepers. At 8.30 they are dressed in blue jackets and white trousers, to wait on the first breakfast—thirty sit down to it. At 9, the second breakfast, fifty more sit down to that; then busy cleaning all the breakfast plate. At 1, a sitting-down lunch for 140, with frequent removes of plates and knives and forks. Cleaning again. At 5, the first dinner, at which they all wait, and again at the second dinner, at 6.15; everything being fresh laid, clean table-cloths, &c., for the second dinner. From 8 to 10 tea, lemonade, drinks of all kinds, are going on in the saloon. Besides all this, the beds have to be made, rooms cleaned, and slops emptied, all through the day, and they never finish till 11 at night. Next I pity the poor black punkah boys—five of these are now daily in the saloon, pulling all day long—they look so tired, occasionally squatting down on the floor, and still pulling. But if these are hardworked, think of the firemen and Sidi boys amidst the pandemonium of the furnaces, 35 feet below decks, where no air can reach them. They are, I suppose, to the manner born, otherwise they could not live in a heat which sometimes touches 150°.

Sunday, 29th Oct. We have entered on the regular Red Sea phase of our voyage. The piano is on deck, and there is music and singing throughout the day and till 10 at night. Many of the passengers have their beds brought up and sleep on deck. The fore part of the deck is impassable at night from the numbers of Lascars and negroes sleeping about and across in all directions. We had Divine service on deck this morning (after the usual muster), the awning and shrouds being gaily dressed with flags, and an Union Jack thrown over the capstan, from which the captain read the service—hymns, with piano accompaniment, a pretty and impressive service, and, I am glad to say, heartily joined in by all. To-night the moon is still more brilliant. I have been leaning over the gunwale looking across the sea towards

Mecca, nearly opposite which we now are, watching the silver wake of the ship and the shimmer of the moon on the sea, everything reminding me that we are in the tropics, and thinking of you and dear Nelly's fireside, and how snug and comfortable you all are, although probably you would like a portion of our 90° of heat. I have been in an incessant bath for 36 hours from the heat exuding at every pore day and night, but I am perfectly well and sleep well also, though you could wring my night-shirt. We shall soon be out of it, I hope.

Monday, 30th Oct. The heat has been greater to-day than on any previous day—90° in the companion and 88° in our cabin; but as we approach the Straits of Bàbel Mandib, the wind has got up, blowing through the Straits as through a funnel, and we contrive to collect the wind by rigging out a towel from our port, keeping it tight by a soda water bottle tied on to the lower corner, which thus acts as a windsail for our particular benefit. We have been out of sight of land for two days; nevertheless, we were visited by an owl yesterday and by a couple of swallows to-day. The sea was here and there covered with flights of locusts to-day, driven out from land, and of course perishing in the sea. Monier has written a capital account of the Suez Canal for the "Times." If it appears, mind and keep the cutting for me.

Tuesday, 31st Oct. A head wind against us, but still as hot as ever. We have passed two separate groups of islands in our run to-day—volcanic and sterile—so sterile and so remote as to make them impracticable for a lighthouse. The navigation of the Red Sea at this point is consequently dangerous; the ports on the starboard side of the ship have been closed owing to a tossing sea, and the unlucky passengers on that side—ladies as well as gentlemen—have consequently been obliged to sleep on deck. We expect to be in the Straits of Bàbel Mandib by daybreak to-morrow. This letter must then be posted in anticipation of the despatch at Aden. Our final stage, six days' run from Aden, will then be Bombay.

Wednesday, 1st Nov. We passed through the Straits of Bàbel Mandib at 5 o'clock this morning. Captain Methven (with whom I have made friends) considerately sent down to our cabin to tell us. I put on my overcoat and hastened on deck at 4.30. The moon on one side and Venus on the other were lighting up the heavens; Orion brilliant over head; the Southern Cross over the starboard bow of the ship, on our left was the high land of Arabia, which gives rise to the name "The Gate;" close on our right was the Island of Perim, of which we have taken possession, and on which was a brilliant revolving light, the channel being only two miles across; our ship, looming grand in this mysterious scene, was holding her own confidently in mid-channel, her spars lit up by the heavenly bodies above us. And so we passed through Bàbel Mandib, or "The Gate of Sighs." I remained on deck till sunrise, and we are now in the Indian Ocean steaming towards Aden, where I post this letter. Tell Ro, Eugene, Harry, and the girls, that they are ever in my thoughts, even in the wonderful scenes which I never thought I should have the good fortune to witness.

SS. "Nepaul," Indian Ocean,
Thursday, 2nd November, 1876.

True to my custom I begin this letter immediately after despatching the last, posted at Aden yesterday, although no mail leaves Bombay, I am told, for a week after our arrival, and that cannot be till Tuesday, the 7th, at the earliest. Never mind, I have something to say about Aden, and the sooner I say it the better. We arrived at that place—place is not the word for it—at that huge cinder yesterday afternoon, and anchored in the bay. Captain Methven did not intend to coal there, but the post office required six hours to arrange about letters, and there was cargo to take in and to discharge. You remember Vesuvius? Well, Aden is a conglomeration of the cones of Vesuvius, the tops all charred and jagged, with deep rugged fissures scored all down the face, from which the gradual crumbling of the burnt-up rock has caused slopes of débris, leaving on the side next the sea but very little flat ground available for man. On this flat, but still raised from the level of the sea, are seen the bungalows and houses of the residents, the jetties beyond, and again more houses dotted round the bay, which sweeps round inland and forms the isthmus connecting the rock with the main land. Directly the ship was anchored it was surrounded by a dozen or more Somali boys, each in his canoe, hollowed out of a tree, wielding a single paddle, all nearly naked, their beautiful skins and forms shining like polished ebony; their weak point in the way of personal ornament being their heads, for whilst some were closely shaved and some were plastered over with a thick kind of yellow pomatum, others had their woolly hair frizzled and screwed up in long tight corkscrew-curls standing upright all round the head, the hair of some of them being dyed yellow. It was our first introduction to savage life as distinguished from Eastern life. These urchins are absolutely at home on and in the water. The moment a bit of coin was thrown out into the sea from the ship, in they all splashed in a moment, and all we saw was a cluster of feet as they disappeared head-foremost beneath the surface in a diving race for the money. The canoes were left to drift about in one direction, half-full of water, the paddles in another. By-and-by up they all came bobbing about like corks, the successful imp with the money in his mouth, and then they all made after their canoes and paddles, getting into the canoes, though not more than a foot wide, with the greatest dexterity, and then baling out the water with their hands, and coming back to the ship for another plunge of the same kind. We landed at 3 in a boat rowed by five of the same race (Somalis)—a handsome kind of negro, but a savage all over, and engaged a queer sort of conveyance—a cross between an American four-wheeler and a phaëton of the time of Queen Elizabeth, drawn by a chestnut Arab pony, to take us to the tanks, about five miles off, for three rupees. The road ran along the bay for half the distance, then zigzagged through a gorge of the rock, descending on the other side into a plain in which is the military cantonment, and beyond again, at the foot of the precipitous wall of cinder, which bounds the cantonment on the other side, are built the tanks, one above the other, intended to collect the precious rain which is said to descend on Aden once only in three years. I can believe it, for the tanks were as dry as they could be—not a drop did they contain. The drive gave us a capital idea of the place, and of the population. Troops of camels were coming and going, laden with all sorts of burthens, a few evidently used as hacks, ambling along at the rate of about six miles an hour with riders, and some were returning empty ridden by naked boys seated on high pummels, their feet resting on the neck of the animal. Then there were bullock-carts drawn by the Indian humped bullock, horses and mules, droves of African sheep, white with black heads and large fat excrescences where their tails should be, mixed up with the most extraordinary medley of human races—Parsees, Fakirs, negroes of every tribe, Hindoos, Arabs, women of all races, some veiled, some not, a few of both sexes dressed in the most brilliant colours; but the savage type prevailed, and the larger proportion of men were nearly naked, and distinguished only from each other by rude ornaments, or by the fantastic arrangement of the hair. These passed us in swarms, throngs, and, to account for the numbers, there were all along the road and in the cantonments whole villages of native houses and huts where I suppose these naked savages live like rabbits. It was an extraordinary sight, both the place and the people. There can surely be nothing else like it under the sun. It did not appear to me that the place was strongly fortified, nor that there were more troops than sufficient to keep such a demoniacal population in order. Indeed, I did not see a single European officer or soldier during our drive. The Parsees have settled at Aden, and form the mercantile portion of the very limited respectable community of the place. We pulled back to the ship at 6, much awe-struck by the sombre yet grand aspect of this gigantic cinder as the setting sun fell upon it. Our crew was again all negroes, steered by a little ebony woolly-headed imp, quite blue from excessive blackness, not nearly so big as little Ebby. As I looked at him seated cross-legged on the edge of the plank which formed the stern of the boat, with the tiller in his hand, as grave and impassive as a judge, I said to myself, "How I should like to take you home with me, you dear little demon,"—and I gave him a threepenny piece for little Ebby's sake. On our return to the ship we found her discharging bales of Manchester piece-goods and taking in bags of gum and elephants' tusks—a good illustration of the change we have ourselves gone through of late. She had taken on board also several native families—Mussulmans and Hindoo, with their extraordinary goods and chattels: their matting, rattan boxes, water-pots, and cooking utensils, gourds, their messes of food—these people I saw grouped on the sheep-pens on deck this morning, the two races being of course separated as carefully as the chief officer could separate them in such a confined space. We also had taken on board three Brahminy cows and several of the African sheep I saw in our drive, and a good supply of plantains, larger and riper than those we get in London. All the ship's dirty linen was left at Aden, and a complete and fresh supply was shipped to serve us to Bombay. The ship is now a little world of itself—English, Scotch, Irish, Portuguese, Maltese, Germans (we have five or six Germans on board going to buy indigo in Bengal), Africans, Indians, Chinese and Arabs. All these living, cooking, eating, sleeping, praying according to their several habits, creeds, and prejudices. Amongst the saloon passengers, too, every class is represented, except the church—we have no clergyman on board. With that exception we are fit to found a colony anywhere just as we are. But I shall not be sorry to be on terra firma again, with more elbow room.

Friday evening, 3rd Nov. The sea the whole of this day has been like glass. It is strange to look on a vast expanse of sea meeting the horizon all round, with a surface like quicksilver. The sun went down in rosy splendour, and after a few minutes of twilight the moon showed herself on the opposite side, rising majestically out of this glassy sea almost as large and as bright as the sun. A broad, flashing bar of silver across the sea connected her with the ship. The eye could scarcely rest on her, she was so large and brilliant.

African Sheep
taken on board at Aden 1 Nov.

p. 30.

The moon and Venus, of all the heavenly bodies in these tropical skies, are exceptionally large and beautiful. The other luminaries do not do themselves the same justice, and I was certainly disappointed with the Southern Cross. It continues hot—thermometer below, in saloon, 80°, but the temperature is fresher than in the Red Sea. It is *dolce far niente* with a vengeance on deck such a day as this. Too many people about, and frequently the piano going, to settle down to read. Plenty of whist parties on deck and in the saloon. Eugene would be in his glory. I lounge, gossip, sketch, read, then stroll to the fore part of the ship, look at the native families huddled together on the sheep-pens, scratch the nose of the poor old horse, bestow the same sympathy on the unfortunate cow, whose calf, poor little thing, has been converted into veal long ago, then caress the mild, kindly African sheep, which we took in at Aden, and these affectionate creatures poke their glossy black heads and lop ears out of the bars of their pens, asking to be fondled. It is a shame to kill them. Look in on the well-arranged mail cabin, where two intelligent deputies of the Post Office, aided by two natives, are busy from morning to night, surrounded by large, open-mouthed bags, sorting the letters for all parts of India, Burmah, China, &c. These men have as much as they can do to get their task done during the run between Suez and Bombay. I have also been down into the engine-room and furnaces, down to the very bottom, under the wing of the chief engineer. Fancy, when the thermometer under the breezy awning on deck is 80°, what the heat must be in the iron avenue below, between eight boilers, each boiler heated by three furnaces! I can tell old Ro that he is far better off as a lawyer than he would be as a Sidi boy. There are worse professions ashore and afloat than that of a lawyer, he may be sure. He may even congratulate himself that he is not my friend on board, the indigo planter of Tirhoot, who has lost, and may lose again, £8,000 or £10,000 in one year by the failure of the crop from drought; or my other friend, the jute merchant, who has a hot time of it, running about the provinces, buying the stuff of country growers and seeing it packed and carried in bullock carts to the different railways, and who is longing for war, that he may at last look for some profit from the sweat of his brow; or my third friend, the captain of cavalry, whose regiment is stationed in Upper Scinde, at Jacobabad, a sandy desert for 100 miles round, retaining a temperature night and day for eight months of from 90° to 100°, the roads being all laid with flags and rushes, the better to carry the traffic, and whose wife told me that every night, when at the station, she soaked her night-shirt as well as her bed in water, in order to find relief from the burning heat at night; or other men on board, in the Service, who are carrying nurses and squalling children back with them to India, to save the expense of putting them out with friends or governesses in England. Knocking about in this way, one sees how hard it is for men who are not born to riches to earn an honest livelihood, even if the fact were less patent at home than it is. There is one man on board, who sits next to me at meals, and whose occupation a youngster might well envy. He is Captain Greig, formerly in the 92nd Highlanders, and now one of the Conservators of Forests for the North Western Provinces. He spends the largest part of each year in tents, moving about through and by the side of the forests which extend at the base of and parallel with the Himalayas, directing the cutting and planting of trees and the management of the forests. This is another name, in fact, for perpetual sport. His entire camp equipage is found for him, including two elephants, on which animal alone he is able to penetrate the dense jungle through which he has sometimes to pass. He said to me yesterday, "Why can't you leave your brother for a fortnight, and come and pay me a visit? You will see life with me, and sport such as very few men who have been in India all their lives have seen. I'll send the elephants down to meet you at" (naming the place), " if you will only write to me a few days beforehand and fix the day." But of course this is impossible. I have been very fortunate in having him for my neighbour at table.

Monday, 6th Nov. We have had a charming run across the Indian Ocean. For two days the sea has been as smooth as glass, with lovely nights. The thermometer keeps at 80° in our cabin, but the heat is not oppressive now. To-day we have a fresh breeze, which just crisps the surface of the sea. The ship is going twelve knots an hour, and the expectation is that we shall arrive in Bombay to-morrow evening, being twenty-four hours before the contract time. We shall have been afloat four weeks all but two days—quite long enough. I am getting tired of the four notes of the engine, one, two, three, four—one, two, three, four, all day and all night; also of the ship smells; also of the cooking, although that art is carried on under the most remarkable difficulties, and due allowances should be made; also of our confined accommodation at night, and the discomfort of making your box your wardrobe, and dragging and digging and diving into it for all changes of clothing, with the heat at 80° at the least; also of the monotony of the last six days, for we have not seen land or a ship of any kind since we left Aden; also (though this involves a sort of contradiction) of the crowd of passengers on deck and at meals. So, all things considered, and not desiring to undervalue the ship, and much enjoyment connected with it, I shall not be sorry to find myself in Bombay. I shall close this letter on board ship, intending in my next to give you all the particulars of our landing. We shall not, I fear, hear from home for a week after our landing. What an age it seems! and how absolutely impossible it is for me to suppose that you may be at this moment freezing or groping your way about London in a November fog! Distance makes one think more of home.

Tuesday, 7th Nov. 7 p.m. We are now within 30 miles of Bombay, and expect to get in by 10 o'clock to-night. We have had a quick and favourable passage all through. Thank God for His care of us. All the passengers are busy packing up and are in high spirits at the prospect of the journey's end. I close this letter, which cannot, however, go for a week, as we have just passed the homeward-bound P. & O. steamer.

BOMBAY, FRIDAY AFTERNOON,
10th November, 1876.

YOU will receive, or ought to receive, two letters from me by this post—one posted from on board ship and this one written three days later. We leave Bombay to-night for Fred. Sheppard's camp at Mehmadabad, and I am anxious to send this off to-day in the possible event of my not being able to post a letter from the camp in time for Monday's mail. We anchored off the Apollo Bunder on Tuesday night about 10, and so brought our voyage to a happy end. It was too late to land that night, but we had the usual amount of amusement looking over the side of the ship at the shore—boats coming and going, and the excitement of an unknown land twinkling with lights at no great distance from the ship. To bed we went that night on board but not to sleep. The steam winch just over our heads was at work all night; and the noises to which I had been accustomed, now in an exaggerated form, coupled with the excitement of having arrived at our destination, kept me awake all night. At 5 a.m. on Wednesday morning I was upon deck just as the "Nepaul" weighed anchor to steam up the harbour to Mazagong, 3 miles higher up. The sun was rising over the Ghauts, and the often-described features of the harbour were presented to my view in their full beauty. Captain Methven saw me in my hasty wraps in the bows of the ship gazing on the lovely scene, and came down from the bridge of the ship and dragged me back with him on to the bridge, where he expatiated and steered and steered and expatiated alternately, until we brought up at Mazagong and dropped our anchor finally. I then dove down (as a Yankee would say) to our cramped and stuffy cabin to give a final touch to my packing before landing. Whilst I was so engaged perspiring at every pore, for there is no sudorific like packing when the heat is at 85°, in walked Lancie Fletcher. This was about 7 a.m. It was very good of Lancie to come and very useful he was. He had brought a boat from shore and his own puttywallah with him. The individual is his office messenger, dressed in turban with a sash and brass plate. With the aid of this man we got all our luggage on deck, and had it passed by the custom-house officers and transferred into the boat, landing at once and avoiding the general scrimmage of passengers and baggage at the landing-stage. Lancie had his dog-cart close at hand, into which he and I got; Monier and Stanley took a carriage, and the puttywallah came on with the luggage in a bullock ghari, and thus we arrived safely at Pallonjee's Hotel, passing through streets affording the most wonderful novelty. In fact, although I thought Aden incapable of being surpassed, we have been going on in a crescendo scale in the way of novelty and interest, and certainly Bombay is the climax of all. What would Mivart say to Pallonjee? Our bed-rooms opened on to the compound, mine was a kind of loose box such as we have at Craven Cottage for the horses, iron rails at the top of the partition open to other iron rails at the tops of other bed-rooms; and although I had a few sporting engravings hung on the walls, some birds had built in the rails in my room and were flying in and out without any fear, whilst a couple of lizards were sticking on to the walls as comfortably as if they were part of the furniture. Outside was the bath-room; Monier and Stanley, who had a double-bedded room close to mine, having their outside bath-room also, and visible to any one passing in the compound were our ablutions in these annexes. A fresh-water bath with soap was such a comfort after four weeks of sticky sea water! The scene after breakfast looking out from the spacious verandah on the first floor of the hotel over the paddy fields, the men and women going to and from a piece of water under us, the primitive water-wheels, and all other moving objects, baffles all description. And what can I say about the native town through which we drove in the afternoon? the variety of form and colour in the native houses, every recess and verandah and roof being full of effect, every shop containing figures and materials for the artist, the extraordinary vehicles drawn by Brahminy oxen, the buffaloes, the water carriers, oxen with water-skins, the strange scenes at all the public fountains, the variety of costumes, the turbans of every shape and colour, no words can describe it. But what struck me most of all was the nude form; thousands of nearly naked men meet you at every turn; they are not athletes, but the native figure, with his brilliant black or copper skin, the natural grace of his attitude, as he is engaged in his trade or is waiting at the fountain with his brass pot on his head or carried on his hip, or carrying his basket of fruit or vegetables either on his head or on a bamboo suspended across his shoulder, or walking easily and briskly along, is a study enough to drive a sculptor wild. The female is draped, but the habit of carrying a burthen on her head has given the whole race an elegance of carriage of which we in England can have no idea. Certainly the nude male form has impressed me as much as anything I have seen here in the way of perfect beauty. Yesterday Monier had engagements with Sir Jamsetjee and others, consequently Lancie called for me in his dog-cart at 6 a.m. and drove me all round the island of Bombay, passing through the woods of Mahim, composed entirely of the date palm, the palmyra or brab, and cocoa-nut. Picture to yourself four or five miles of the hothouse vegetation of Kew Gardens and you have the Mahim Woods. Here and there a native garden with ferns, fan palms, bigonias, poinsettias in profusion. The last-named grow 8 or 10 feet high as a common garden plant and are now in full flower. By 11 we were at his bungalow on Malabar Hill, a very choice little place on an eminence, with a nice peep of the sea and everything very complete. Here I was introduced to Gertrude, who was waiting for us in the verandah, and I passed the rest of the day with them. The dinner was quite first rate, a Portuguese male cook cooking in an outhouse over a charcoal fire, with a few copper pots and pans just placed over the open fire. Nothing could be better. In the evening I returned to Bombay, and this morning I have been driving about the town, and amongst other things buying my resai, a basket, some cartridges, powder and shot, and preparing for our visit to Frederick Sheppard. We have also engaged two servants, one, Canjee Rama, at thirty rupees a month, the other, Naryen Lalla, at twenty-five rupees. Both experienced goodlooking men, dressed wholly in white with red and gold turbans, and naked feet and earrings, rather different from Smith and William in Green Street. The Thakore of Bhownuggur has been very civil, and his agent has been here to tell us that relays of horses will be provided for our visit to Kattywar, which will include Pallitana. Yesterday Lancie took me to the Pinjera Poll, or hospital for diseased and aged animals, established by Bunniahs, who insist on the sanctity of all animal life, a virtue carried to the most absurd extreme; and we also looked in, at my request, at the stables of two of the chief native Arab horse dealers. What would Anderson or Rice say to his Parsee rivals,—for though the owners and importers are Arabs, the dealers are Parsees? We entered as bold as brass. The Parsee Anderson came forward with his salaam, "What kind of horse do you want, sir?" "Oh!" said Lancie, "my friend (pointing to me) wants a charger." He accordingly took us round the sheds. The horses are not in separate boxes, but are tethered by head and heel ropes in long rows under open sheds, so that you see the beauties at one glance all in perspective. We chose one. "Have him out," said I. He was unloosed, a native put a bridle on and then jumped on barebacked and trotted and cantered the animal up and down the avenue, the Arab owners with their hoods and camel-hair cloaks looking on to see what the customer would say. "What price?" "3,000 rupees;" and then we had others out. "What do you ask for this?" "2,000," and so on. There was nothing less than 1,200 rupees, and very few were above 14.2 in height, out of, I suppose, 100 horses which we saw. It was a pretty and a novel sight, but for mere horse flesh I would rather have a good English hack, and the price would not be half what they ask here for an Arab. This afternoon we are going with an order from Sir Jamsetjee to the Towers of Silence, and the carriage is now waiting to take us there.

CAMP-MEHMADABAD, GUZERAT,
Wednesday, 15*th November*, 1876.

THE English post is not expected to arrive till Friday, and we have been therefore without any home news except your letters at Suez. Nevertheless I must begin my letter for the next mail, because unless I seize a vacant afternoon, such as that I now have, I may miss my opportunity altogether. We left Bombay by the mail train on Friday night. That same evening we met Sir Jamsetjee's secretary, at the Parsee Cemetery, on Malabar Hill, generally known as "The Towers of Silence." Irrespective of the interest attached to the locality as a sacred spot, the view from the terrace gained by a long flight of steps looking over Back Bay, the town and harbour of Bombay, with the islands in the harbour and the range of Ghauts in the distance, is the most commanding of any in the neighbourhood. But the chief interest rests in the peculiar rites of the Parsees in the conduct of their obsequies. At the time of our visit a large funeral procession was approaching the towers. It consisted of the bier on which was laid the body of the dead man, covered only with a sheet and carried by four bearers belonging to a sect especially devoted to that service, who live and intermarry entirely amongst themselves. Then at an interval of 100 yards followed a priest leading a large white dog. The secretary, who was with us explaining the philosophy of the rites, evaded all questions about the dog. We understood that at the moment of the corpse entering the tower the dog was made to lick the face of the corpse. Behind

One of the Towers of Silence Malabar Hill Bombay
Funeral Procession
10 Nov. 76.

F 40.

the dog followed about 100 Parsees, all dressed in white, some priests and some relatives and friends, walking two and two, some of the couples holding a white handkerchief between them in token of communion and sympathy. These all advanced to the portal of the large round tower (one of five or six of similar construction) on the top of the hill overlooking the sea, and then wheeled round and suddenly returned to the Fire Temple which they had passed on their way to the tower, and distant some half-mile or so from it, leaving the bearers of the bier alone to enter the tower and deposit the corpse on the stone platform within its circumference. This the bearers did, removing the sheet which had hitherto covered the corpse, though the act was not of course visible to us, and then, emerging from the portal, they proceeded to a well within the precincts at no great distance, where they stripped and washed themselves, throwing their clothes into the well and putting on fresh clothing. No sooner had they left the portal when troops of vultures which had been gathering and seating themselves on the parapet of the tower, with an unerring instinct of what was coming, pounced down on the body and tore off the flesh, reducing it to a perfect skeleton, as we were told, in half-an-hour. We learnt from the secretary that the dry bones are eventually thrown into a hole in the centre of the circumference of the tower, there to mix with the bones of all those, rich and poor, who have gone before; the bottom of the hole, as well as the drains communicating with it, being laid with charcoal; the theory of the whole process, founded on the tenets of Zoroaster, being that no impurity of any kind should be permitted to defile the mother earth. In the meantime the priests and relatives of the deceased had been worshipping in the Fire Temple; and all having afterwards washed their hands at the entrance to the temple, they went away down the steps as they came. Here is a ground plan of the tower:—The

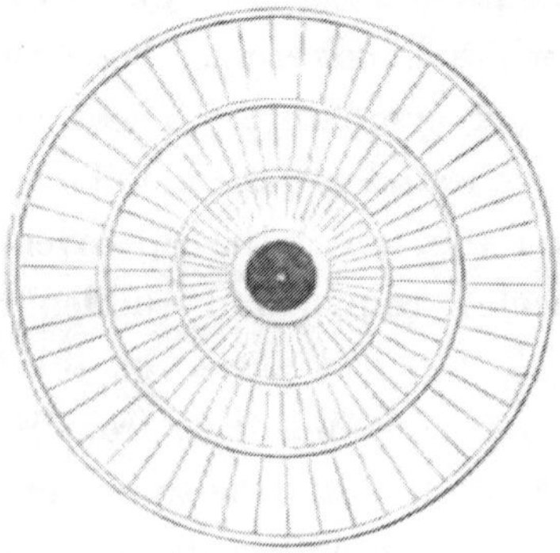

outer circumference is for the bodies of males, and is known by a Guzerati name, signifying "good deeds;" the intermediate circumference is for females, and is known by another name, signifying "good words;" and the inner is for children, and is known by another name, signifying "good thoughts." The hole in the centre is that into which the dry bones are eventually thrown. So particular are the Parsees that no filtration of impurity should by chance descend from the platform into the earth, that several slabs of stone were rejected in the construction of the tower because they had veins of quartz running through them, and it was supposed that these veins might decompose in the course of centuries and so make a channel from the platform to the earth. The setting sun lit up the tower, as the procession left it, throwing the dark brab and cocoa-nut trees surrounding the tower into grand relief against the glorious sky. It was an impressive scene.

On our return to the hotel we separated our luggage, leaving our heavy things there and taking with us only our bags for light marching order. The railway carriage was less comfortable than I expected. It was only half a saloon, adapted for four only, so that we had only one berth to spare, not more than enough for our traps, and the cushions and corners were dusty in the extreme. Night, of course, prevented our seeing anything until long after we had passed your native town, Surat. The sun was rising on Broach as we slowly and cautiously crossed the long temporary bridge over the Nerbudda, the former bridge having been swept away during the last rains. You may fancy how I gazed on the bright town as it glittered in the morning sun on the opposite bank of the river as the train moved on, stopped and felt its way across the creaking bridge. I said to myself, "Is it possible that I was born here, that I have been here before, have seen this beautiful river, the same groups of cattle and villagers on the now contracted sandy banks, the same scenes in fact that I am now looking on. It surely must be a dream." But the present is always too strong for me, although it may be less poetical than the distant or the future, and so we got out of the carriage in the flesh to breakfast at Baroda; and eventually, at 11.30 on Saturday morning, arrived at this station, very grimy from the hot and dusty journey. The three large and turbulent rivers, namely, the Tapti, the Nerbudda, and the Mahi, which, rising in Central India, run into the Gulf of Cambay, are formidable difficulties in the way of this line of railway; the iron bridges, in each case, are more like viaducts, spanning in dry weather a vast dry bed of sand in which there is no holding for the piling, but which bed in the rains becomes a rushing torrent, against which the iron piles offer a feeble resistance, and, consequently, frequent damage occurs at these points. Arrived at Mehmadabad, we found Fred. Sheppard waiting for us, and he conducted us to his tents, pitched in a field adjoining the station, and here I was introduced to camp life for the first timo. I was at once shown into my own sleeping-tent, one of the group, divided from which by a canvas screen is the bath-room. Imagine the comfort as well as the novelty of a bath under such circumstances, after fifteen hours of heat and dust. Now of what does the group of tents consist? First, there is the drawing-room tent, about twenty-five feet square, double walls and roof, and fitted inside with tables, chairs, sofas, carpet, and every other convenience. Leading immediately from this is a kind of club-room tent, pro bono publico. Then Fred and his wife have three smaller tents for themselves. I have my tent apart, with iron bed, carpet, wash-hand stand, table, &c., from which there is a wing for the bath. Monier and Stanley have their tent, the clerks and officials have their tent, and Fred has his office tent. The cooking is all done in the open under a tree, but there is a dwarf wall of matting round the fires. The sideboards, with the necessary paraphernalia on them, are outside the door of the drawing-room tent, and also in the open. The horses are tethered with head and heel ropes under trees in the open, and bedded on rice straw; there are six or seven horses, each horse having his own groom, who sleeps at his side, also of course in the open. The goats for milk, poultry, and farmyard generally congregate round the tree which represents the kitchen. All the tents are pitched under mango trees, and the effect of the encampment, the horses tethered in the open, the camp fires of the kitchen, and also of the retinue, and the goats and animals and carts and men moving about, now under the shade of the trees and now in sunlight, is original and striking. The retinue is large; house servants, mounted guard, sepoys, policemen, grooms, add to the life of the scene. The table and cooking is excellent—a complete menu every day,—and the dishes as well served as if in London. Three times I have been out with Fred shooting—I ought to say with Fred and his wife, for she always goes with him and walks and rides and goes through an amount of fatigue which few women would be up to. On these occasions the native keepers and beaters are sent off before daylight to the ground intended to be shot over. There are about a dozen of them, most of them three parts naked—some with red turbans, some blue. We three, that is, Fred, his wife and I, are up by 6, just at daybreak. We have tea and toast and fruit. Then we mount, Fred's wife having most kindly placed her own Arab at my disposal. The sowar (or one of the mounted guard) precedes us, and we gallop along the soft sandy country roads to the place of rendezvous, from 5 to 8 miles distant. There we find the beaters and three grooms ready to receive our horses, and off we are on foot through the crops and fields after quail. All is new to me, as you may imagine, the operations of agriculture as we walk along, the Guzerati bullocks ploughing or drawing the primitive wicker cart, the natives gathering the crops, or preparing for threshing on the mud floors in the fields, the crops themselves, the wonderful variety of animal and bird life,—birds of prey of all sizes and colours, foxes, jackals, monkeys, parrots, doves, birds of varied plumage, black and grey, scarlet and grey, blue and yellow, the saras or magnificent grey crane with scarlet head, peacocks,—all these we put up in our walk. It is wild shooting, indeed; but quail is the object of our walk. Fred is a dead shot, and generally gets his twenty or thirty brace of quail to his own gun in the course of our two hours' walk. By that time the sun has become too powerful, and we beat back to our horses, which have been moving about with clothing on them during our absence, sit down for ten minutes for soda water and whiskey, mount and gallop back to the camp—all being over by 10 o'clock. Then I adjourn to my tent, strip off my soaking garments, lie down on my bed with my bath towel round me, and so soon as I am cool plunge into my delicious bath. The middle of the day, after breakfast at 12, is reserved for writing or reading, or in Monier's case for seeing visitors, and at 4 we either drive or walk out till sunset: dinner at 7.30, after which we emerge from the tent and sit before a wood fire, which crackles in the field outside. It is a free and independent life—not, however, without drawbacks. The heat continues oppressive, the thermometer 88° in my tent in the middle of the day; the dust of the village roads both when riding and driving is annoying; animal life around and in the tent is almost as prolific and varied as that we meet with for sport. All night long sleep is more or less murdered by discordant noises; the howling and laughing of jackals and hyenas; the shriek of owls and strange night birds; the hoarse whoop of monkeys,—all aggravated by the fear that some of these may walk into your tent at night, for all is open. Inside the tent smaller tribes of insects are patent to the eye if by chance you look for any lost article on the carpet with the help of the candle. I amused Adelaide (Fred's excellent wife) by insisting on taking my umbrella to bed with me as a weapon of defence. She herself is as plucky as possible and cares for none of these things. She is passionately fond of horses. This afternoon she drove me in her tonga and pair of ponies to Kaira—preceded by a mounted sowar—distant 6 miles. The tonga is a rough kind of curricle, two wheels, pole, and wooden bar across, well adapted for a pair of ponies and for country work, and stylish withal. The stable consists of these two ponies, two Arabs, and Fred's big Australian horse, all rather spicy and good of their kind. We propose leaving this on Saturday for Ahmedabad. Evan James is here with his tents. He is now Postmaster-General of Bombay. We remain at Ahmedabad till Monday and then viâ Baroda to Broach, where we shall stay a day to enable me to see our old house there, crossing afterwards to Gogo for Kattywar.

Dakor, Thursday, 16th Nov.

We have had two expeditions to sacred places. The first to Wurtal, distant 20 miles from our camp, and the second to Dakor, to-day, from which latter place I now write. Wurtal is situated 5 miles from the railway station. It is the head-quarters of the Puritan sect of Hindoos, followers of a certain holy (and, perhaps, dirty) man yclept Swami Narayan, who died fifty years ago only, but who (so like the Romish system of canonization) was supposed after his death to have been an incarnation of Vishnu, and is worshipped accordingly. The Maharajah of Wurtal had notice of our coming, and on our arrival at the station we found waiting for us an elephant caparisoned with a silver howdah and crimson trappings, a palanquin, several bullock gharis, and a mounted guard of half-a-dozen ruffians on rats of horses, with a host of beggarly retainers on foot. Eager for novelty I got on to the elephant, which was made to kneel down for the purpose. Monier preferred the palanquin; our servants were stowed away in the gharis, and the procession moved forward amidst a cloud of dust and the delight of the bystanders. But oh, the elephant! the howdah was divided into two parts by a partition, and it was impossible either to sit or lie down in either compartment; the jolting backwards and forwards brought the partition in sharp contact with my spine, and the holding on, with the powerful sun overhead, threw me into such a violent perspiration that I said, "Hang the dignity, I have had enough of it, I'll get down!" So I stopped the beast, slid down, after he had again knelt, and transferred myself into a ghari. Wurtal is a temple surrounded by a large quad, in which live about 300 Sardoos or religious men, devoted to celibacy, and to preaching and meditation. Here, again, there is a strong affinity to monasticism. We were received most courteously by the Maharajah in grand durbar, and Monier obtained explanations from such of the Sardoos as understood Sanskrit, more especially on the precepts of Swami Narayan, who, so far as I could learn, appears to have been a reformer and good sort of man. It was interesting from the striking analogies which presented themselves between their ideas and those of the Romish church. We returned to the camp in the evening. This place (Dakor) is another sacred shrine belonging to a more sensual sect and which attracts vast numbers of pilgrims periodically. To visit it requires two days. Adelaide Sheppard has been so good and thoughtful about it—all our beds and bedding, tables and chairs, our food, linen, soap, knives and forks, servants, sepoys, &c. have been sent forward by rail; and what was before an empty kind of hut with mud walls and chunam floor has been carpeted and furnished, bedding put down, and everything made ready for our occupation of it for two days, including to-night. It has been a regular migration. I could not have believed it possible. We have had an excellent breakfast. F. Sheppard is with us on this occasion. Hot meals, clean table-cloth, napkins, &c. as if we were at home, and I am now occupying the hot hours of noon by writing this to you. At 4 o'clock we are to sally out to see the splendid temple, tank, &c. about a mile off. But I will not weary you with descriptions of sacred buildings, which, some grander than others, are pretty much alike everywhere. We were here also to have had an elephant and procession, but we have countermanded it. I fear, however, we are in for a durbar. This kind of life—I mean moving from home in force to empty houses with only a floor and bare walls—is common in India. No one except those accustomed to it, like F. Sheppard and his active wife, could organize it and think of everything as they have done now. We have such numbers of servants and sepoys about us, and that relieves us personally of much trouble and they are so subservient. "Do this and he doeth it" is illustrated every moment of the day. The heat and fine dust are very oppressive, and we could not exist without plenty of willing help. We return to camp to-morrow, sleeping in this funny hut to-night. P.S.—We have walked into this stronghold of fanaticism and superstition and fraudulent priestcraft, accompanied by our guard of sepoys. Fred would not enter the temple;

Fakirs
at Dakor
17 Nov 1876

p. 48.

and afterwards, when he joined us at the durbar and learnt that the priests had made us take off our shoes before ascending the steps and had refused us admission to the idol, he broke up the durbar (very properly) and refused the presents, much to the dismay of the priests who surrounded us. The whole way to the tank and temple we were followed by a vast multitude of people as well as by the elephant. It was an extraordinary spectacle,—these vast crowds being more or less under the influence of the temple, and the idol well worked by the artful priests for their own profit. It is Lourdes over again, only in a grosser form. We could not have seen a more striking instance of Hindoo fanaticism.

BARODA, WEDNESDAY,
22nd November, 1876.

I BEGIN this letter at 6.30 a.m., seated at the dressing-table of my bed-room at the Residency, with the thermometer at 65° only, having had my chota hazzaree, or cup of tea and toast, and my cold bath, and therefore all as comfortable as if I were at Dolly in July. My last letter was posted at F. Sheppard's camp on the day we left it. I did not like to delay it till we got to Ahmedabad for fear of missing the post. We were only an hour by train to Ahmedabad, the minarets of which I saw in the distance long before we entered it. There at the station we were met both by Mr. Tagore, the native judge at Ahmedabad, who had entered the Civil Service by competition, with whom Monier was to stay, and by Evan James, whose guest I was to be; so we each went off on our respective hooks—Evan and I in an humble ghari to his tent—Monier in a flashy barouche with gaudy-coloured servants and a pair of rats of horses hugging the pole in the most un-English fashion. I was glad to be independent and with Evan, who did all he could to make me at home, having put up a tent expressly for me. We hired the ghari by the day,—not a bullock carriage, but a queer little covered two-wheeled trap, into which you entered from behind, lifting up the cross seat at the entrance, then flopping down on a cross seat opposite, ducking your head or sticking it out of the window to avoid the top of the roof until the first cross seat is shut down, and then both passengers settle down on that and face the horse—for horse it is. Evan is perfect in Hindustani and knows Ahmedabad well; consequently in this little conveyance we scoured about the town and environs seeing everything. Evan always calling out to our willing driver "Geldie, geldie," *i. e.* quick, quick; and he, in his turn, shouting out to the crowds in the streets to get out of the way. It is the custom to address anyone happening to be in the way by his trade or calling, "Heh ghari wallah," "Heh chokra," "Heh ghora wallah," and so on; and if the occupation of the obstructive be not conspicuous, then it becomes "Heh jan wallah," or traveller or wayfarer generally, but always in a sharp loud voice. It is needed. The teeming crowds in the provincial towns of Guzerat completely choke up the thoroughfares, but the men in their white dresses and well-arranged red or green turbans, the women in their graceful sarees and bangles and ornaments, and holding themselves like queens, and the poorest classes in (what I like best) their natural buff or rather black, will bear a favourable comparison with the dirty fustian-clothed mechanics and labourers in our own provinces, most decidedly. There are some beautiful remains of Mahommedan art in and around Ahmedabad—the Jumma Musjid, the mosque and tomb of Ranee Seepree, the mosque and tomb of Shah Alum and others; and all have the same distinctive beauties,—that is, rejecting the deformed gods and goddesses with which the Hindoos are so fond of covering their temples, they stick to geometrical designs of the most graceful and elegant kind. It is in the perforated stone panels, the sharp undercutting of the ornaments, the beautiful tracery, the variety of design in the ornaments, that these buildings are so conspicuous. The vibrating minarets of the Jumma Musjid were destroyed by the earthquake of 1818 (I fancy I can remember that earthquake), but several pairs of minarets belonging to the other monuments remain and give character to the town. Another feature of the town is the cantonments about three miles off. These consist of large open spaces, approached from the town by good roads and handsome avenues of either tamarind or banyan trees, and flanked by the soldiers' lines, cavalry stables and barracks, mess-rooms, hospitals, tennis courts and other buildings, all built with verandahs, and other adjuncts suitable to the climate. We drove out there two mornings at 6 o'clock to see the troops at exercise, and very pretty it was. Evan's tents were pitched in an open space within the walls of the town, at one end of which square was Mr. and Mrs. Tagore's house. Every morning at 4 I heard the creak, creak of the wheels of the well close by drawing up the water in leathern buckets by two pair of bullocks, the water finding its way along channels parallel with the roads and then scooped by women and boys stationed at intervals with metal dishes and dashed on to the roads, altogether a very primitive mode of watering the roads. But everything here is primitive. I bought some gold lace or trimming of a merchant who came with his pack to the door of the tent. I asked the price; he said he could not tell, he sold it by weight. We had to send himself and the lace and our own puttywallah to some authority in the town who possessed scales, and all returned with the lace and a long sum in arithmetic and a certificate. I asked him if the lace was made in Ahmedabad. He said "Yes, come and see." Evan and I accordingly drove through the back ways of the town, and in a little dirty courtyard of a little dirty street we were shown a ladder. We ascended the ladder and came into a hovel with a mud floor about 8 feet square, in which were seated on their haunches a couple of naked men working on gold lace and embroidery with the rudest frames. You couldn't have conceived it possible that such beautiful work could have proceeded from such tools; and the men appeared so contented and so glad to see us, and produced their rude self-originated designs, our chief light being through broken tiles in the low roof.

Driving home to our tents one night, after visiting some

p. 52.

of the mosques and tombs, we were attracted by a large assembly of respectably-dressed turbaned men singing in a new and well-lighted and well-ventilated church-like building. We stopped the carriage and entered. It was a meeting of the Prarthama Somaj, or advanced sect of Hindoos, Deists in fact, for prayer and singing, Mr. Tagore presiding. There were three professional musicians seated on the floor, one with an enormous kind of banjo, who led the singing, another drummed on two tom-toms, and the third played a rude kind of fiddle. There were about 250 or 300 persons present, who all joined heartily in the singing, and there were two galleries in the upper part of the building, screened off carefully in front, but which twinkled with lights inside, and evidently contained ladies. Evan James kindly obtained for me a native translation of the hymns which were being sung by the assembly. Forgive me if I send you a few verses by way of sample. You will judge from the sample of the religious opinions which are rapidly gaining ground amongst the educated Hindoos of the present day—

> "Let us sing His name who has formed this worldly house,
> Where His mercy never ceases, and pours uninterruptedly down;
> Thy consecrated food maketh thy worshippers glad.
> Oh, Lord! thy glory is endless and pure;
> Thy glory holy sages sing with heart cure,
> And they sing it until fatigue makes them free.
> Oh, Lord! thou art the root of mercy: who can match thee?
> Is there any other friend equally beneficent in chivalry?
> Not in chivalry alone, but in adversity and prosperity,
> Except Thee, O Lord! there is none.
> Oh, God! bestow thy mercy upon us, and let thy mercy secure to us
> Eternity, in place of the mortal grave.
> Prevent all our sins;
> Shine in our hearts: what else may we ask of Thee?"

I am not responsible for the translation, which may nevertheless be considered first-rate as compared with the run of translations from the vernacular by natives. Immediately prior to the singing, Mr. Tagore delivered an address in condemnation of caste, all being in keeping with the reforming spirit of the meeting.

We left Ahmedabad by the 12 o'clock train yesterday, arriving at Baroda at 3. Mr. Melvill, the Chief Commissioner or Resident, had invited us all to the Residency, and a carriage was waiting for us at the station, and he himself greeted us under the portico of the palatial house, which goes by the name of the Residency. He is a Bengal civilian, but was one of the three English Commissioners who sat in judgment on the late Guickwar. On the deposition of that villain, a boy of twelve, related to the reigning family, was selected as the successor to the throne. Sir Madhava Rao was appointed his dewan or prime minister, and Mr. Melvill, the Commissioner, rather to the disappointment of the Bombay civilians, who look on Baroda as part of their patronage. These two men have therefore the charge of the boy, and practically govern the state. They have got an English tutor for the boy, who is trained to ride, to wrestle, play cricket, &c., besides book learning. He is always one day in the week at the Residency, and frequently with the young English officers in their camp, so as to give him manly notions instead of leaving him to be the puppet of the wives and mistresses of the old villain Guickwar, who still swarm in the palace. Soon after our arrival at Baroda, Mr. Melvill's carriage drew round, and, escorted by some of the Bombay lancers, he and our three selves drove into the town, distant a mile, the guards turning out and drums beating at every guard house and gate as we passed it. Baroda is far more native than any town we have yet seen. Not being under our dominion it has nothing European about it. Here in the main street we met lots of irregular soldiers on horse and on foot; men with cheetahs or the hunting leopard,—men with trained hawks,—men in all sorts of oriental costumes,—elephants, camels, then a clatter of horses and the young Guickwar passed us on horseback at a swinging trot, escorted by a large party of irregular horsemen. Flash again, and the Rajah of Oudeypore came by in his carriage and four with a similar but differently-dressed escort; greetings and salaams were exchanged between Mr. Melvill and his escort of lancers and the other magnates. Every man in the streets salaamed to us as we passed. The streets were more crowded even than usual for Guzerat; the gaily-coloured alcoved and balconied houses swarming with people in the alcoves and balconies, besides the crowds in the streets. In this way we drove along and back to the Residency before night. After dinner a cloth was spread over the matting of the spacious hall, and in came a troupe of native musicians with their extraordinary native instruments, and treated us to a most original performance, quite perfect of its kind, all squatting on the floor on their haunches, and themselves absorbed in the music. The Prince of Wales was Mr. Melvill's guest for five days last year, and these men performed before him. I will undertake to say he never saw or heard anything of the kind before. I have occupied the bed-room on the ground-floor in which the poison was administered to Colonel Phayre; they call it the poison-room; but the Colonel is alive and kicking, and consequently there was no ghost in the case; rats, bats, frogs and jackals of course all through the night, but I am accustomed to such noises by this time.

Thursday, 23rd Nov. Mr. Melvill sent me into the city yesterday morning to sketch, under an escort of police, whilst he and Monier had an audience with Sir Madhava. Sketching in a native town needs a strong escort of police; without it you must expect to be surrounded by a crowd of at least 1,000 people. In Baroda we were protected, except from the stinks—open sewers run all through the town, parallel with the streets. I took my seat with my back against a door leading into a small paved courtyard; horrible whiffs came across me occasionally. I opened the door, and there, within a couple of yards of me, was a cow on her side dying by inches, her eyes picked out and body covered with flies. When an epidemic visits the town the people are carried off like rotten sheep, and no wonder. We returned to the Residency to tiffin, took leave of these kind hosts, and left for Broach by the 2 o'clock train, arriving at Broach at 5 o'clock. Mr. White, the collector, a Haileybury friend of Monier's, was in the districts, but most kindly placed his bungalow at our disposal, and here we are ensconced in clover, with the building all to ourselves—our meals served, and every hospitality shown to us as if he were here in person. It is a roomy, cool, pleasant bungalow, and I am enjoying the quiet after the Baroda Residency. I have been to the Umjad Baugh this morning and into the room where I suppose I was born. What a dream it all is! The house will not, however, exist much longer, for a cotton factory company have got possession, and will, perhaps, pull down all the present buildings and adapt the ground to a second Manchester.

Friday, 24th Nov. Last night I embarked on board an open native boat to visit the Kubir Bur, the great banyan tree, 15 miles up the Nerbudda. Monier would not risk the night air. We slept on board and were well bitten for our pains—the boat anchoring for the night in the river after we had punted 10 miles. At 5.30 this morning, still quite dark, except from Venus, who was shining like a moon, we got into a small kind of canoe, and, frequently grounding, reached the Kubir Bur at 9 o'clock. It was a failure, and not worth the bother of the night journey. Is it not strange that I am equal to all this bodily fatigue as if I had only left Umjad Baugh twenty years ago instead of——. We returned

Parsee Fire Temple at Broach 25 Nov 76.

Whiteman & Bass, *Litho to the Queen*

p. 57.

this afternoon under sail, with a fair wind, and on arriving at our bungalow here found all your letters. The situation of Broach is picturesque, standing as it does on high ground, immediately overlooking the Nerbudda. All rivers are interesting in India from the crowds who frequent their banks, especially the women in bright clothes of all colours going and returning with two or more lotas or shining copper or brass vessels, one above the other, on their heads. I can scarcely believe that my dear old mother passed the greater part of her married life amongst these scenes. We leave to-morrow for Surat, and it will depend on what we can learn there about the means of crossing the Gulf of Cambay whether we go into Kattywar or not. The sun is very hot still in the middle of the day—too hot to be comfortable—and every day is the same. It is not possible to sketch in such heat, and I fear you will be disappointed at the few rough things I have done.

BOMBAY,
28th November. 1876.

HERE we are back again at Pallonjee's Hotel, and it seems very much like coming home-again. We have given up Kattywar, as you may infer from our being again so soon in Bombay. The fact was that Monier had been suffering, and did not feel equal to roughing it. To cross the Gulf of Cambay from Surat, about twelve or fourteen hours of sea, was a doubtful experiment, and the means of transit lay between a native open boat, called a bunder boat, and a tug steamer, which began to run yesterday only, having come from Bombay for the purpose the day before. Of the bunder boat we saw samples in the Nerbudda. It is a kind of Chinese junk, with the stern cocked up in the air, the planks apparently sewn together, a blob of mud in the stern, to serve as a receptacle for the fire for cooking, the single mast carrying a tattered lateen sail, with a crew to match. All very well for a cargo of cotton, which may equally well be delivered this week or the next, but not very comfortable for the professor, afflicted, or supposing himself to be afflicted, with any internal derangement, however slight. The steamer required more respectful consideration. But she was new to the station—had only arrived in the Tapti on Sunday; she was only 120 tons; the crew were all Mahommedans; we knew nothing about her or about the men; all our provisions must be laid in by ourselves and our cooking done by ourselves; and she was to start with the tide at 4 a.m. on Monday morning —confessedly requiring fourteen hours to cross from Surat to Bhownuggur, on the other side of the bay. Monier is now quite well, but on Sunday he was not sure of himself. So, all things considered, we determined to give up Kattywar and return direct from Surat to Bombay. But you have not yet heard of our being in Surat. My last to you was from Broach. At Surat we were most kindly received by Mr. Birdwood. He is a married man, but his wife and children are in England. He had staying with him the second assistant, Mr. Frost, and young Frederick Goldsmid, with whom, of course, I immediately claimed friendship. Mr. Birdwood is the Judge at Surat, and occupies the Adawlut bungalow—the very house which, I presume, your father and mother lived in for so many years, and where you were born. Is it not so? It is the perfection of a house for this climate. It is a quadrangle of about 100 feet square, open, of course, on all sides, within which is an inner quadrangle, supported on and divided from the outer by three wide arches on each of the four sides; and this inner quadrangle is again divided by arches into a dining and drawing-room, so that the effect is excellent as well as the space and ventilation. From off this main building branch the bed-rooms, accessible by broad passages—the whole being on the first floor. Below is the Adawlut or Court in which the Judge presides, and in which there is ample accommodation for him, his registrars and officers, the vakeels or pleaders, suitors, witnesses, &c. One is impressed both above and below with the spaciousness and suitableness of the building. Then from the verandahs in the first floor there are extensive views of the Tapti, looking down the river and up it. I was of course exceedingly interested in the whole building, connecting it, as I did every hour of the day, with your father and mother and yourself. Indeed, the whole atmosphere of Broach and Surat is redolent with memories of days gone by, and if the sins of the fathers are visited on the children, so their good deeds, as in our case, reflect honour and credit on their posterity. The names of my father and yours are remembered and honoured to this day in Broach and Surat; my father's book on Broach being, as Mr. Birdwood told me, a text-book in his Court at this present time. On Sunday we went to the English church, both for the early service at 7.30 a.m., and for the evening service at 5.30, the service on both occasions being performed by Mr. Birdwood. After morning service I went to the cemetery, but could not recognize any names I knew. The punkah was going during both services; the thermometer rising every day to above 80° in the shade even now. We remained with Mr. Birdwood till Monday (yesterday) evening. I employed Monday in sitting with him in his Court, then driving out to the Artillery camp about a mile off, and an amusing scene it was. Besides the guns and the artillery horses, all tethered by head and heel ropes in the open, there were twenty elephants belonging to the commissariat, and about fifty camels, on the same camping ground; these, with their wild attendants, the men's bedding (for each man slept by the side of his elephant or camel), the equipages and trappings, cooking utensils, fires, tents, commissariat bullocks, European and native soldiers going to and fro with forage, native women with water-pots, all bustling and moving about, formed a very striking scene. Young Beaufort of the Artillery showed us all round. By-and-by we saw an elephant "packed," as they term it—that is, a huge thing like a mattrass strapped on to his back, and then something else on to the top of that. Frost, who was with us, asked, "Hullo, what's that elephant packed for?" "Oh!" replied Beaufort, "he's only going to the railway station to fetch my portmanteau." Imagine the expense to the country of all this paraphernalia and all these camp followers to accompany half a battery of artillery in time of peace! And accordingly we saw the huge beast, with a couple of mahoots, on our way home, scuffling along the road to the station just before our vehicle, swaying from side to side in order that he might bring one eye to bear on his right rear at one step and the other on his left at the next, packed, and accoutred, and bedizened, taking up the whole of the road—and all for young Beaufort's portmanteau, which any native woman would have brought out on her head for three annas! In the afternoon of Monday I amused myself by buying some Surat toys; they are rather grotesque but very original, and are made only in Surat. I am getting together several packages at King's, a few things I purchased at Ahmedabad and at Surat jails, nothing first-rate, but genuine, as I saw them made by the prisoners; three or four white marble animals I met with to-day here in Bombay, carved at Jeypore; some native shields made of the skin of the nielghau, painted in Indian patterns at Ahmedabad; and I shall collect in like manner as I go along—nothing costly, but as Indian as I can. On Monday night at 8 o'clock we left Surat by train, and arrived here at 4 a.m. this morning. I am writing this at 9 o'clock at night, and am tired and must now go to bed.

Thursday, 30th Nov. We have been to-day to Elephanta. The governor placed a steam launch at our disposal. Montague Fawkes and Robert Anderson, the two aides-de-camp, called yesterday to acquaint us of this civility, but we were out; Robert Anderson, however, turned up this morning and accompanied us in the launch. We embarked at 8 a.m. Nothing could be more lovely than the sail up the harbour in the morning sun, or than the Island of Elephanta itself. Springing out of a vivid undergrowth of vegetation rose the elegant brab tree, now singly, now in clusters, a straight stem to the height of 80 or 100 feet, and then a graceful head of palm leaves crowning the top. Other islands dotted about the harbour, the picturesque native craft with their thatched cabin aft, thatched with palm leaves falling almost into the water, and with their white cotton lateen sails gliding about between the islands, and the distant Ghauts beyond, coloured with tints which no paint-box could reproduce, combined to make it a scene of enchantment. The excavated temples have been often described, and the figures are no doubt majestically treated, but I don't know or care enough for Hindoo mythology to feel interested in these monsters. I was absorbed in the natural scene, and saw much more to fascinate me looking out of the dark entrance of the temple on to the panorama of palm trees, blue sea, islands, and exquisite distance, than into the niches and recesses where dwelt Brahma and Siva, and all the other miserable brutes of the Hindoo pantheon. The return voyage was equally beautiful, such hosts of shipping and such life of all kinds on the surface of the sea. We landed at 2 p.m., and hearing in the meantime that the mail boat had come in, I rushed home to the hotel, ignored a posse of snake charmers and conjurers three parts naked, who were performing in front of the hotel, ran upstairs to my bed-room, where I found and devoured your budget of letters. Is there such a thing as fog or snow? I cannot believe it. Here we have every day the same climate, a shade too hot for me—for the heat rises to above 80° every day in the house and in the shade—but in other respects perfect. I dined with L. Fletcher and his wife yesterday, and drove home by the light of a full moon all through the cocoa-nut wood which spreads between Malabar Hill and this hotel—such a fairy scene. Beneath this cocoa-nut wood the natives live in their low mud huts It was such a striking scene by moonlight that I have sent Monier out to-night to the same spot in the carriage to look at it.

MAHABALESHWUR,
6th December, 1876.

No one can say I am a bad correspondent, for I do fire off lots of letters, not only to my own relations, but to friends, and that whilst my thoughts are occupied by the distracting scenes around me. But I want to thank you for your letter, and so I sit down to write one expressly to yourself. I often long for you two girls to be with me, and with a few drawbacks you would both enjoy the life. What are the drawbacks? First, the heat: even now the heat in the middle of the day,—not here, for this place, as you know, is one of the mountain sanitariums of India, but in the plains,—is excessive and stops all exercise from 10 to 4, except under the penalty of a wet shirt. Then the dust, and especially in the railways—not to be wondered at, seeing that no rain falls for months. It is an impalpable white dust, and all the more penetrating. Then, first cousin to dust, the glare. I am sure that my eyes have aged more from these two causes the last two months than during the previous ten years. Well, then comes the animal life, especially at night. Musquito curtains are some protection, but not against noises inside the bed-room and outside. The scuffling of rats can be distinguished by the Britisher; but there are whizzes and groans and chirps and squeaks peculiar to an Indian night, and which cannot be identified as coming from any English animal. I have not done yet. The accommodation at the hotels makes one creep a little now and then. In the first place, there is not a fastening on any door or window to any bed-room. Every door and window is expected to be left wide open all through the night. It was only the other night, at Poona, a huge dog walked into my bed-room after

I was in bed and had put the candle out, and I had to bellow at him to get him out. Then the carpets are uneven and spread on straw or some substance, which suggests a refuge for destitute fleas beneath; and the ceilings, instead of being plastered, as with us, are covered with a kind of sacking, which bags down and occasionally breaks away. This forms an upper storey for insects, &c. Stanley was asking Rama (our man-servant) only to-day at dinner—"Rama, what are those things like cocks and hens which run about all night in the ceiling of my bed-room?" "Oh, master," Rama replied, "they not cocks and hens—we call them wambas: they have mouth like a rat, and always live up there;" not very comforting if one of these things were to lose his foothold and flop down on your bed in the middle of the night. More than once I have chased lizards out of the bed-room. But you never wash in your bed-room; leading out of it is an annex, generally with a mud floor, in which is a large wooden tub, which annex is accessible from the outside as well as the inside. Whether you are in the tub, or preparing to get in, or just getting out, the bheestie, or attendant for that special department, walks in from the outside at his will. If you are out of the tub he draws a cork at the bottom of it, and out runs the dirty water over the mud floor and through a hole in the wall into the street or garden, as the case may be. The bheestie is naked and so may you be. It does not signify a straw, you don't look at each other. My annex in this hotel is approached from my bed-room by three mud steps leading down into it, and I must stoop my head to clear the door. The floor is uneven mud, and there is a mud rim round the place where the tub stands to prevent the dirty water from going away except through the proper channel. I have given you a catalogue of some of the drawbacks. The novelties and excitements, per contra, I have detailed in many of my home letters.

You, as a housekeeper, would be delighted with the servants—the men-servants who wait at table, so beautifully dressed, generally snow white, with scarlet or crimson and gold turbans, such gentlemen in manners, so attentive and courteous—the men cooks (generally native Portuguese), clever and managing and proud to please. There is no trouble about their food. You pay these men some 12 or 15 rupees a month, and they sleep where they can and find their own food and everything else; up always before 6 to bring early breakfast, and ready all day outside the door whenever you call. At any moment the master inside his room may call out "Boy," or "Qui hi!" Immediately the response comes, "Sahib!" and the man is at the door. No drinking, no swearing, no Sundays out, no followers, no overdressing. The cooks go out daily marketing and arrange the dinners themselves. The mistress only has to say six to dinner to-day, or, even an hour before dinner, to say two more coming, and everything is arranged without a single word. Harry would have been amused at the sight I saw on the Green, in Bombay, the afternoon before we left it—a Parsee eleven at cricket. The Parsees are a go-ahead people in Bombay, are wealthy, and imitate the English; but their physique and dress would, one would have supposed, have been unsuited to cricket. No, there they were hard at it, with a large marquee for their friends, who appreciated the play, and applauded a good bat or a good ball. It was very funny to see them with their Parsee hats, muslin petticoats, and coloured trousers, batting, and running, and fagging out. When I say coloured trousers, remember the colour is of the brightest, and the material satin—either crimson satin, or yellow satin, or violet satin—not business-like, Harry would say, but the wonder is that Asiatics should play at any game which requires exertion. And yet to see the native women at work one would not blame the nation for slothfulness. The poor women are always at work, sometimes navvy work, earth-work on railways; but when they are washing, or drawing, or carrying water they never look more graceful; always delicately covered in a brilliant saree, which shows enough, not too much, of the form, their style and carriage is most attractive, sometimes balancing two or three bright brass lotas on their heads, with both arms uplifted, sometimes a large brass lota empty on the hip, or a child carried on the hip, a leg on each side, sometimes a basket or bundle of canes or vegetables on the head, then the arms and legs often covered with bangles, ears jewelled—altogether the female Indian figure is quite a picture. At Broach, the other day, I saw a naked father at the door of his mud hut with a naked little brat across his knees, boring holes in the little brat's ears, the mother sitting opposite and helping; the poor little creature was screaming and yelling, and the father was boring away till the operation being, as I suppose, over, he put her on her legs again. I called her to me, and by her father's desire she came toddling to me, as naked as when she was born, with only a single bangle on one of her little ankles, and I tried to comfort her with a few copper pice, much to the father and mother's amusement and delight. It is no ordinary boring, remember, but holes all along the top of the ear, as well as in the lobe; the earrings extend all round, and frequently weigh down the top of the ear to an unpleasant extent.

Poona, 8th Dec. Tell Ro that all news concerning Craven Cottage, and the horses there, is intensely interesting to me. How men can gallop across country here after hog or any other game I cannot understand. The ground is baked as hard as a brickbat, and full of deep fissures, with ragged ends, hard and sharp as a saw. No horse, I fancy, but the Arab could do it; their legs are as hard as nails, and they are extremely intelligent. It must be dangerous work even with Arabs. I have just been down to breakfast alone (Monier having gone off early to the Kali Caves) in the public room of the hotel; there were eight persons present, each with his own servant behind his chair—each servant dressed in white, with red sash, and red and gold turban, and naked feet. I had mine, Devram, who was dressed in the same way. His sole object is to study every want, and to anticipate it, and, in the meantime, with a dexterous flourish of his napkin, to drive away the flies which may settle on your head. There were ten double French windows in the room, opening down to the ground; every window was wide open. The punkah was not going this morning, but it generally is; the windows and doors of my bed-room here, last night, were wide open all night, not so at Mahabaleshwur, at least, not to the same extent.

I should tell you that one morning we drove to the Hindoo temple of Parvati (the wife of Siva), situated on an eminence about three miles from Poona, and approached by a long flight of steps. Two of the Brahmins of the temple spoke English fluently. They at once admitted that the idols which they showed us were merely representations or symbols of the one Supreme God, and not objects in themselves for worship; the idols were intended only for the ignorant. Over the sacred bull, which almost always faces the entrance to Hindoo temples as the symbol of creative power, was a large bell. I asked "What for?" "We wake the bull when we ring it." I said, "Wake him now." The Brahmins grinned. I continued, "Wake him, and let him drag our carriage back to Poona, and I will give you a hundred rupees." They grinned again. Monier asked them if they went through such and such ceremonies, the duty of all devout Brahmins. "No," they replied, "we don't." "Why not?" "Because we are sinners." They both pestered us for "favours." I said, "Do you, the priests of the temple, condescend to beg?" They replied, "We ask for the temple, not for ourselves." "Humbug," I replied, "it is the rupee you worship; take down that image of Siva, and put up a rupee instead." They seemed to admit I had hit the nail on the head, being well aware that the whole thing was a cheat.

MAHABALESHWUR,
6th December, 1876.

I COMMENCE this letter seated in the spacious verandah of the hotel here, 4,200 feet above the level of the sea, temperature 60°, looking right and left on projecting spurs of the hills covered with trees in full leaf, and beyond, on successive ranges of mountains, some of the most fantastic outline, the view ending with the Indian Ocean, 50 miles off, near Rutnagherry. It is a marvellous scene, and no wonder that this place is one of the sanitariums of India. Does it not seem strange that at this season, the winter here as well as in Europe, all the trees should be in full leaf—as full as in July in England? The plateau, approached from Poona by a steep ascent of three hours, and, extending, when the top is gained, for 10 miles westward, appears to end here, and it does not end in a straight line but in a series of bays or deep indentations, and to each spur or point there are excellent roads. Standing on these spurs or points you look down nearly perpendicularly on the valleys below from a height of 2,000 feet, intersected by sharp ridges of hills at every conceivable angle, some of them covered with brushwood,—others, where the basalt has cropped up, broken into strange forms of every variety. There is no mountain scene in England or Wales with which I can compare it. The peculiar geological formation of the Konkan makes it a scene of itself. There are first-rate roads, not only to these points which are 12 or 14 miles apart, but in every direction—the colour of the roads a red sandstone, skirted by tall ferns and wild flowers, especially a colossal kind of wild mint of great fragrance, and the trees often meeting overhead. It is a lovely as well as a healthy spot, and would be so in any part of the globe, but, coming from the parched plains of Poona, the contrast is the more striking. We were advised to travel by night to avoid the heat. Accordingly we engaged a barouche and pair to take us three and one of our men-servants, and to start from Poona at 9 o'clock on Sunday night, the owner sending on relays of horses according to the custom, for the total distance is 75 miles, the charge to be 35 rupees, tous compris. We packed ourselves very well in a good, roomy carriage, and I remarked at the time that we had a good, well-bred pair of horses—chestnuts—to start with. Our turbaned driver and our man Rama were on the box, our three selves inside and a turbaned ghora-wallah behind—all very promising, under a brilliant moon. We soon cleared the twinkling lights of the Poona shops, and, after a few miles of quick going, began a long, winding ascent through arid, treeless hills, ending, at the summit, in a tunnel. We emerged from the tunnel on to a valley on the other side, more effective under the bright moon by contrast with the tunnel, and were commencing the descent when one of the chestnuts (who had before showed a slight symptom of restiveness) began to jib. It was the horse on the near side. If we had been in a Hansom, the London cabby would have humoured the animal, spoken to him, waited, or perhaps backed him a bit, or turned him round. But our turbaned driver had only one remedy; and whilst he lashed the poor brute furiously, the turbaned ghora-wallah jumped off from his perch behind and seized the off horse by the head, dragging him forward. That horse jumped on, whilst the near chestnut, resenting the whip, jibbed viciously. The consequence was that the carriage was forced suddenly and violently on to the dwarf parapet, a stone wall 2 feet high, which protected the road on the left from a drop of about 60 or 80 feet into the valley below. In a moment the near horse, the jibber, toppled over the parapet, hung for a second or two by his harness, and, the traces breaking, down he went, rolling over and over into the valley beneath. We could distinguish him by the moonlight lying on his back, but, to our surprise, we saw him after a short time get up slowly and walk away limping down the valley. I turned to the carriage and saw that the pole had snapped in two. The off horse had become dreadfully frightened, and would have done more mischief in a moment. I really was the only one of the whole party who knew anything about horses. We had all jumped out of the carriage, which, but for the dwarf parapet, must inevitably have been toppled over with the horse. The two native men were stupefied, and, like all Asiatics, gave themselves to their fate. Stanley knows no more about a horse than he does about a megatherium, and Monier got away to a safe distance, and, seated on the dwarf parapet about 20 yards off, lifted up his voice and contented himself by calling out in a melancholy tune, "Krāb, krāb, krāb!" which, I was told afterwards, is the Sanskrit for bad, bad, bad. He meant that the driver was bad, ghora-wallah bad, and horses bad. I told Rama instantly to seize the remaining horse by the bit, and showed him how to hold him by a firm hand, one on each side of the bit. I then unloosed the traces, and, having freed that horse from the carriage, I made the ghora-wallah get over the parapet and descend into the valley in search of the fallen brute. In the meantime I examined the pole, cut a couple of green twigs from the only bush near us, and contrived a splice with some rope fortunately in the carriage. But what was now to be done? We were 10 miles from Poona, 11 o'clock at night, and 4 miles from the village where the next relay had been sent. Neither of the natives would ride the sound horse back to Poona. Rama, interpreting, said, "Men say that horse won't let no man sit on him." "Very well," I replied,

" clap him into the carriage; the pole will do for the present, and let him drag the carriage singly to the village." No sooner, however, did the animal touch the pole than he began to kick furiously. He was demoralized, and trembled from head to foot, and unless he had been taken out would have kicked the carriage into splinters. By this time the ghora-wallah was seen through the dark coming up the road with the limping horse, which he had found some way down in the hollow. There was no help for it. I took hold of the sound horse, and told Stanley to lead the other. Monier rose from his seat on the parapet and got into the carriage; the two natives and Rama dragged it and Monier. I led the sound horse and Stanley the other; and in that way we accomplished the 4 miles to the next village. On the road we met droves of bullock gharis, the drivers of which stared at our ghastly procession, and no doubt prayed to Vishnu to be delivered from all evil spirits, for we must have looked like a cross between Winkle and his stolen horse and some of the Hindoo deformities, by the misty moonbeams' struggling light, partially obscured by the fine dust caused by the traffic. We got to the village in due time, and a hot dusty walk it was. There the two natives sat down on their haunches, and would have done nothing if Rama and I had not dug the spurs into them. Between us we respliced the pole, and with the aid of a lantern mended the harness with rope and twine, and made a pretty tolerable refit of the whole concern, encouraged by some hot tea we found in a mud hut with a board nailed on to it labelled "The Star of India," indicating that it was a public. The fresh pair of horses were regular old jades, and I never looked on old worn-out screws with more complacency in my life, for I still had my misgivings about the splice in the pole and the rope-pole strap. However, the fresh pair were at last stuck in, and at 2.30 a.m. we were off again, arriving safely at the Travellers' bungalow at Wai to breakfast at 10 a.m. instead of 6. Very pleasant it was to rest here and have a wash, after the night's toil and dust and anxiety, and then wander out to see the whole population on the banks of the pretty little river Krishna, the women in their brilliant sarees bathing and washing, and themselves enjoying the water as much as we did. From Wai commences the three hours' ascent I have before referred to. It is a very steep ascent, though the road is well engineered along the face of the mountain range, on which stands the plateau. Here horses and their attendant evils and dangers were discarded, and the carriage was dragged up by twenty-five coolies with ropes, and precious hot work it must have been for them, their naked black bodies shining again with sweat. But they did it well and without beer; the only encouragement being their own yells, shouting out to each other at intervals for a spurt. All these fellows were included in the tous compris of the thirty-five rupees, but at the top I held out a couple of rupees, and got them all together, and said, "Now for a scramble;" they grinned, but would not scramble. Rama said the two who got the coin would divide it equally amongst all. Their three hours' hard tug over, they came forward to us, and, lifting their hands, said "Salaam, Sahib," and down they all went to the plains below, having earned perhaps four annas each, or not quite sixpence each. Now contrast this with the English navvy! At the top we had horses again, and drove along the level for ten or twelve miles through a well-wooded country of the same character as this, arriving here at 6 o'clock on Monday evening. On these subsequent two days we have been driving about in a tonga to the different "points," enjoying the foliage and vegetation, and the exquisite temperature of these uplands. We return to Poona to-morrow, and this time will do the journey by day.

Poona, Friday, 8th Dec. We returned to this place from Mahabaleshwur last night, a day earlier than we intended, to enable Monier to devote to-day to the Kali Caves, two hours by rail back on the Bombay line, but secretly, I believe, as much to get our English letters, which we knew would be waiting for us here on our return last night. We left Mahabaleshwur at 6.30 a.m. by the same barouche, and after a pleasant drive, though warmish towards the middle of the day, we arrived here at 6.30 p.m., exactly twelve hours en route. "Letters come?" was the first question we asked of our second man, whom we had left behind, and who came to meet us at the door of the carriage, "Bhōt, bhōt, plenty, plenty," was the answer. Upstairs we went to our rooms, and certainly on the table there were heaps of newspapers, also letters from natives to Monier, and some from King & Co., Goldsmid, &c. to me. But, to our dismay, no English letters. We knew the mail must have arrived from the newspapers—where could the English letters be? We interrogated our Parsee landlord, and sent specially to the post-office, but no letters nor any tidings of any. I was restless all night in consequence, and resolved to telegraph to King & Co. to-day. Monier went off early to the Kali Caves; I remained behind by my own wish, and also to look after our lost sheep, and further to arrange telegrams to Hyderabad, in the event of there being no reply from Sir Salar Jung, for no reply had been sent by him. Judge of my relief when at 8 o'clock this morning, whilst I was downstairs preparing to go off myself to the post-office, in walked the peon with King & Co.'s thick envelope containing the English letters. Why they were delayed I cannot ascertain; but I am only too glad to have got them to give myself any further trouble. Is it possible that England has been suffering from gales and fogs and cold? These perfect days and cloudless skies, day after day the same, preclude the very idea. We were charmed with Mahabaleshwur. It is not the season for it; the hot weather is the season, but it could not be improved upon as we saw it. On our way back to Poona we examined the place of the accident by daylight. I find I have understated the drop over the parapet. It is a fall of 100 feet. How the poor horse survived I cannot imagine. It was a narrow escape. By daylight back we enjoyed the continued stream of people and vehicles of every kind and description which passed us on the road, gorgeously-dressed men in brilliant clothing, naked men with only a string round their loins, women with their bright-coloured sarees and shining brass lotas on their heads, gipsies with their buffaloes and paraphernalia, fakirs, sardoos, sellers of Ganges water, pilgrims with flags, camels, horses, bullocks, bullock gharis with their shining naked drivers straining and tussling to get their carts out of the way. Indeed, what surprises me more than anything is the dense population of India. It is simply a gigantic ant-hill.

MADRAS,
11*th December*, 1876.

SINCE I wrote to you from Poona we have traversed 7C0 miles of railway at a stretch. Madras is 8C0 miles from Bombay, Poona is about 100 miles from Bombay, consequently from Poona to Madras, which have been our limits of late, it is 700 miles, and a good long run it is in this hot and dusty country without stopping. For half the distance we had a good saloon carriage, that is to say, we left Poona at 9 o'clock on Saturday night and arrived at Raichore at 1 p.m. yesterday, Sunday. For that distance we travelled by the Great Indian Peninsular Railway, and our carriage had a washing-closet, &c. and good sofa beds. Thence commences the Madras line, and we had to change into a single compartment of a carriage like our English carriages, and performed the rest of the journey uncomfortably, arriving at Madras at 7 o'clock this morning, having been two nights and a day en route. Both Monier and I however stood it very well. It is an uninteresting journey and well performed at night. The only incident worth recording was the passing at the entrance of the Nizam's territory of the whole of his camp on their way to Delhi. His highness himself and his minister Sir Salar Jung had already crossed us in the railway in advance. Most reluctantly we were compelled to give up Hyderabad, owing to Sir Salar's absence at Delhi. It would not have been safe to go there without protection. We saw the kind of sight we had missed in the retainers who were hanging about the station where the Nizam's camp was—Mahommedans, dressed in bright soldier-like costume with swords and daggers, and they say these swaggering fellows walk about the streets of Hyderabad with their matchlocks and fuse ready lighted. Baroda, which we saw, was a native city of the same character, but Hyderabad beats it hollow. However, it could not be helped, and we had no alternative but to proceed direct to Madras. There was a famine, we were told, in and about Sholapore, extending to the whole of the Nizam's dominions. We saw no instances en route of human suffering, only a general appearance of sterility in the land, railway trucks laden with grain on the sidings, and herds of cattle in the fields evidently in the last stage of starvation,—poor creatures, mere skeletons. Well, on arriving at Madras station we found Sir William Robinson's carriage waiting for us, and were driven through the spacious approaches of the town to his beautiful house, where I occupy a small bungalow in the garden all to myself, very quiet and independent. Thoroughly to appreciate a cold bath you must first go through the ordeal of a railway journey in India. I told Sir William on meeting him at breakfast that he did not yet see us as we were. Was not Naaman told to wash three times in Jordan? If so, how appropriate the prescription! The white impalpable dust of the East will not yield to one scrubbing. Judge of our surprise on being told by Sir William at breakfast that the famine in Madras was tenfold worse than in the central districts. He said that a worse famine had never occurred within his experience of thirty-five years. That in Bengal last year, I think in Orissa, was, to use his own words, "a mere amusement" for the officials compared to the work which had to be done here now. With this information fresh in our ears we started in a hired carriage for a drive to the town and by the sea shore to witness the celebrated surf which breaks on the shore, not so much at this season as during the monsoon. Here along the shore and close to the pier we were brought at once into immediate contact with startling evidence of the famine. Thirty large steamers were anchored in the roadstead discharging rice brought from Calcutta. Without straining the figure I may say that literally there were mountains of rice in bags on the beach already landed and heaped up. Barges and surf boats were plying backwards and forwards between the ships and the shore still unlading; the railway on the pier was in active work passing trucks on to the shore laden with bags to be added to the accumulated mountains. Hundreds of native carts were arranged side by side on the shore, being promptly laden and sent off into the interior with these bags. And then the moving mass of populace on the shore, the able-bodied actively employed in the transport—and it was a study to see these naked men in every possible attitude which can exhibit the human form to perfection—the weakly, including the women and children, hanging about with baskets or small tin pots to collect the scattered grains of rice which had escaped from the bags, sometimes in the interstices of the sleepers of the railway or the planks of the pier, sometimes on the sand of the sea shore after the bags had been heaped up. Frequently we saw women scrape up handfuls of sand and winnow them in a basket to separate the few grains of rice from the bulk of sand. Frequently we saw them and the children take advantage of a small accidental hole in the bags, squeeze the hole, furtively extract a few grains, hide the half handful in their waistbands and then run away. There were head men on all the heaps of bags and all around armed with canes to prevent depredation, but it went on all the same. The beach swarmed with people and mostly of the destitute class. We were told that they had come from the villages in the neighbourhood, where their natural food had entirely failed them, to endeavour to pick up what they could in the capital. At all events, there could be no mistake as to their condition. Every grain of rice was of the greatest moment to the hundreds of old persons, women and children we saw congregated on that shore to-day. Accustomed in London to appeals from professional beggars on flimsy pretexts, which one discards in a moment, I was shocked to witness the undisguised evidence of gnawing hunger all around me. On returning home I questioned Sir William Robinson more carefully on this serious matter. He said they were feeding 10,000 persons daily already, that the area of famine extended to 15,000,000 persons, and that they were only on the threshold of the calamity, which nothing would avert except a cyclone with a rainfall of 15 or 20 inches at once. Soon would come the water famine, which cannot be alleviated by any means or by any precaution. Then the cattle would die by thousands. He took the most gloomy view of the situation, and said they had four months of growing destitution to look forward to. This is indeed a dreadful thing, realized and brought home directly to one's feelings as I have seen it to-day. But enough of misery. The city of Madras cannot bear comparison with Bombay. The flat and uniformly straight line of coast and the dead level on which the city stands is a lamentable falling off from Bombay, with its magnificent harbour, its promontories of Colaba and Malabar Point, the noble sweep of Back Bay, the distant Ghauts. There is not a single geographical feature of interest in Madras, although there are wide roads and open spaces in every direction. The native is different here from the native in Bombay; they are more aboriginal here, more black, at least, more universally black with woolly hair. The women, too, dress differently here, they wear no bodice,—the pretty little ornamented bodice is wanting and with it the support to the figure, and the saree is not worn over the head as in Bombay but thrown over the shoulder. The native female figure, the perfection of grace when carrying the lota on the head, as in Bombay, deteriorates here, except, perhaps, in a very youthful instance, and then it is "when unadorned adorned the most."

I should not myself care to live in this capital, which to me presents no attractions. Even the sea fails to give it interest. The surf is grand, and the passage of the surf boats, even at this quiet season, is something novel and exciting, and the catamarans are peculiar to the coast; these latter are merely three logs of wood lashed together with rope; on these logs stand two naked men with planks for paddles, and they face the surf and preserve their balance on the logs in the most marvellous manner, rising and falling with the waves and guiding their extraordinary craft with great skill and daring. The men wear a little conical cap of platted straw and nothing else. The shore, however, just now is a scene of remarkable excitement on account of the famine as I have already detailed.

OOTACAMUND, NIELGHERRIES,
Sunday, 17th December.

MAHABALESHWUR is rather more than 4,000 feet above the sea. Here we are 8,000. I am glad to have seen and to have been able to compare the two sanitariums of Southern India. We left Madras by the 6 o'clock train on Thursday evening, having been most kindly received and treated by the Robinsons. We found the Madras Station en fête for the Nawab of Arcot, who was going to Delhi by the same train and would travel with us to the junction. His followers, dressed in all the colours of the rainbow, swarmed on the platform and gave our start from Madras a very Indian complexion. Madras is, in fact, very Indian—the people are less mixed, and the vegetation is more tropical, as is natural, seeing that it, and the whole line of country we passed through thence towards Beypore, is not more than 11 or 12 degrees north of the equator. But I should be sorry to live in Madras, and I left it without regret. It is on a flat dead level, and the air felt to me heavy and tainted and sadly deficient in oxygen. We arrived at the little terminus of the branch line which leads to the base of the Nielgherry Hills at 10 o'clock on Friday morning. Since daylight we were able to appreciate the tropical nature of the foliage and vegetation through which the line passed: as an instance of which I may tell you that the fence on both sides of the railway was composed of one unbroken line of aloes in full vigour, some of them in flower, the whole 300 miles—a formidable fence, too, when the plant puts out its solid spiky leaves as it does in this climate; nothing can approach it. We were gladdened also for some hours before we alighted by the sight of the lovely Nielgherries. The name signifies blue mountains, and they are aptly so called. White fleecy clouds, a novelty in this country, rested on the tops, and reminded me of Wales. Orders had been sent on from Madras to have two tonjons, or sedan chairs carried by coolies, ready at the base of the hills, and two ponies. Monier and Stanley were to have the two tonjons, Rama (the servant) and I were to ride each a pony. I have a horror of being either dragged or carried by men when God has blessed me with health and strength, for which reason I walked up the Ghaut at Mahabaleshwur whilst the carriage was dragged by coolies. For the same reason I objected to the tonjon here, and insisted on a pony, whatever might be the heat of the sun. Arrived at the base of the Ghaut we had a good breakfast, and then separated our luggage, leaving our heavy things below at the station. Every package has to be carried up on the head of a coolie, and weight, therefore, becomes a question of moment. At the base we found the two tonjons as ordered and the two ponies, together with the contractor himself, who does all the carrying. Monier ensconced himself in one tonjon, and I waited to see if Stanley would resist the temptation of getting into the other. My example conquered. Luckily there was a third pony ready, and he discarded the tonjon and got on the pony, seizing the pommel, and exclaiming: "Oh, oh! if it kicks, mind, I shall be off"—so much the more merit for him. But as all three ponies had been up and down the Ghaut daily during the season very little kick had been left in any of them. So the contractor, Stanley and I, all mounted, ascended the Ghaut, and Monier followed in his sedan and escorted by Rama. What a magnificent ascent it was! ten miles of steep riding, the high scarped mountains towering above us on both sides of the pass, whilst the path wound through the most lovely varied tropical foliage—palm trees of all kinds, including the slender areca or beetle nut palm, the bella donna creeper, with scarlet fruit as big as an apple, orange, bamboo (an elegant tree when in full growth), cactus, aloes in flower, tree ferns, poinsettias 8 and 10 feet high, wild roses, coffee plant, &c. In every direction flitted birds of bright plumage, amongst them a variety of the bird of paradise. It really was a ride one might dream about; but I could hardly believe the evidence of my senses, the scene was so grand and glorious. We were three hours on horseback making the ascent, which by my aneroid reached the altitude of 7,000 feet. If we miss Delhi and the northern cities of India we come in here by way of compensation for tropical foliage and vegetation such as the north cannot boast of. The ascent of the Ghaut was an unrivalled specimen of the kind. Arrived at Coonoor, the midway sanitarium at the top, the road thence to Ootacamund runs sufficiently level to admit of wheels, and after uniting our forces and our baggage, which had been dispersed amongst the tonjon, ponies and coolies, we packed ourselves all together in a four-wheeled carriage and drove on the same evening to Ootacamund, 12 miles from Coonoor—the road ascending all the way. It was strange how completely the tropical vegetation was left behind at Coonoor, and for the rest of the drive we had chiefly the eucalyptus or Australian gum tree, which has been largely planted in the upland district; and here, in and around Ootacamund, we have whole hedges of wild geraniums, wild roses and tree rhododendrons. There is a hedge leading to this hotel of at least 100 yards in length continuously of geraniums in full leaf and full flower and at least 6 feet in height; and in the two pony rides we have had on the hills, the last two mornings, we saw beautiful tree rhododendrons 25 or 30 feet high, covered with lovely crimson flowers. I have gathered the seeds of some of these, intending to sow them at Dolly. And yet I cannot understand how geraniums and roses can flourish so luxuriantly at this altitude and in this temperature. We have fires in our sitting-room and in our bed-rooms, double blankets on our beds; and this morning, as we sallied forth on our ponies, the hill sides were covered with hoar frost. Here is a contrast in the course of twelve hours from the heat and dust of the plains below, where open windows, punkahs day and night, musquito curtains, dust and heat, were the order of the day! I do not wonder at the governor and his council and staff, and every one else who can, shifting their quarters from hot and unwholesome Madras for six months of the year to this exhilarating climate and picturesque locality. Monier says he prefers it to Missouri, for the latter place was subject to icy cold winds from the snowy range, whereas the climate here is equable. The big game, which an old Indian friend of mine used to enlarge upon in his day as abounding in these hills, has been a good deal shot down; but a herd of elephants was seen about two months ago not far off, and some gentlemen just returned from an expedition about 10 miles off, told me they had killed sambur, a large kind of deer, and had come across the "pug" of a very large tiger and the disturbed sand where he had been rolling himself. One of them said to me, "Come out next year and we promise to show you some really good sport with large game." This would be more exciting than our brace of grouse at dear old Dolly, and not so troublesome or expensive, Eugene, as a river in Norway. If I had guns and rifles with me at this moment I could have grand sport here amongst bears, cheetahs, sambur and other large game, by making friends with the old Shikarees of the place. Ootacamund is situated in a basin, but not in a hollow—that is to say, the basin is large enough to admit of hills and undulations within it; and the residences are detached and scattered about on all these undulations, which are well planted with the eucalyptus and evergreens of fine growth. There are drives and rides in all directions;

pains having been taken by the government to make the place enjoyable as much for the governor himself and the members of the government, who practically live here, as for the general residents. The habitations range from 7,500 to 8,000 feet above the sea, and the rides on horse or pony back conduct you easily to an elevation of 9,000 feet. We rode up to that height ourselves yesterday morning before breakfast, with a fine fresh Champagny breeze greeting us all the way up, and yet in the middle of the day there is a July sun, making an umbrella desirable by way of shade. It is out of the way of the post, and that is one objection. The bags are carried all the way from the base of the hills to this place, about 25 miles, by dawk runners, three or four men at a time, in relays, and with the bags they carry sticks with metal rings on them, jingling these as they run—rather a barbarous mail in these days of steam. We have enjoyed our sanitary visit here. Each day we have had long rides on ponies. To-day we were out from 7 a.m. to 4 p.m., taking our breakfast with us to the bungalow of a coffee planter about 6 or 7 miles off, situated in a nook on one of these high hills, from whence we looked down on the vast plains and jungles of the Mysore country, with Seringapatam in the distance, from a height of 3,000 or 4,000 feet. It was in these very plains that Lord Hastings caught his fever when out shooting last year, and where he died. But what lovely weather we have had here—such a blue sky, such atmosphere for the mountains and distances, and such an exhilarating breeze—every day the same! I send you an orange blossom plucked from a tree in the open air to-day, and the petal of a geranium flower from the hedge I have before mentioned. We drive to Coonoor and descend the Ghaut to the plains to-morrow.

OOTACAMUND,
18*th December*, 1876.

YOU would have been amused and delighted by the troupe of native jugglers which presented themselves before the portico of Sir William Robinson's house by order the other day—a pack of rascally-looking naked fellows, most of them with only a tattered cloth round their loins, but otherwise stark naked—there were about a dozen men, two or three women, and some children. The men took different parts, sleight-of-hand men beginning the performance—and these were the most wonderful of all. They squatted themselves down on the hard gravel, close to the steps of the portico on which we, the gentry, sat, and all around them were the servants of the establishment. Their appliances were of the rudest—a tattered bag to hold the cups and balls, an old clothes basket, a few bamboo poles, and some rolls of dirty cotton cloth, and odds and ends of that kind. After one of the men had gone through the cups and balls, and had brought out of his mouth several large stones, spitting them out one after another, without putting his hands to his mouth, every stone filling his mouth, the naked fellow behind him came forward to my feet with a round stone as big as a marble, and placed it on the step, opening both his hands wide to show that they were empty; he then put one hand over the small stone for a second, and instead of the stone, there on the step were a couple of live scorpions; he took up the scorpions, opened his hand, they were gone, and the small stone only remained: without moving for a moment from the spot, he placed his hand, covering, as I thought, the stone only, on the step close to my foot, the stone was gone, and, instead, there were three live scorpions and a live snake. Here was a naked fellow, with no bag or basket, with only a string round his loins, away from his companions, and within my touch, and surrounded with eyes on all sides. He retired, and another man came forward, and sitting down, balanced a short sword on his forehead; whilst so balancing, he put a thread and separately four small glass beads into his mouth, the beads being rather smaller than a pea: he put his hands behind his back, and then with his tongue, balancing the sword all the time, threaded the beads on the string, and spat them out all threaded. Another took a reed, spun a top, and transferred it to the end of the reed, which he then balanced on his chin, and at command the top gyrated vertically, became apparently motionless, or wabbled, and in a moment, without any effort on the man's part. Another passed a rough rusty sword, full two feet long, right down his windpipe to the hilt, and an iron hook through his nose and out of his mouth—not pleasant to look at. Another, and he was a Hercules, took up a granite stone with his teeth by a rag passed round the stone, which was about 15 inches square, and jerked it backwards over his head. I do not think I could have lifted the stone with both hands. Another handed me a precious hard cocoa nut to show me it was hard and sound, and I rapped it hard against the stone step to see if I could break it. He then threw it high up in the air, and down it came on his head, smashing the cocoa nut into fragments, and covering his head with the liquid. A little girl stuck two straws into the sand, and bending her body backwards till her head was just over the points of the straws, she seized the ends with her eyelids, and thus drew the straws out of the sand. Then they went through the celebrated mango trick. On the gravel, just before our eyes, they heaped up a little mound of earth, into which they put a mango stone, and then covered the mound with a ragged basket as big as a washhand basin, having first watered the earth with a tin cup of water. This was left for a few minutes, and they then covered the basket with a dirty cotton cloth. The naked manipulator then appeared to fuss about a little with the cloth, but it was only a narrow slip of cloth, and he himself was naked, and was close to us on the gravel. All the time he was talking a jargon of Hindostani and bad English, and his companions were joining in; the dialogue over, he drew off the slip of cloth, uncovered the lid of the basket, and there was a small mango tree shining with freshness, with fruit as big as an apple growing on it. He pulled up the tree out of the earth, and with it the stone, with a good long fibrous root attached to it, and handed all to me. I broke off the fruit myself. It was growing, and the fruit adhered to the stalk and was full of perfume, and the plant itself full of life and freshness. The basket trick was equally wonderful. The woman was tied in a net and put into the basket just before us on the hard gravel, the basket, like the other appliances, being of the rudest kind, and just big enough to hold the woman. Then came the usual tests of stamping in the basket, and poking a sword through it. I fancy the clever woman must have doubled herself up so as to admit of this being done without hurting her, but the illusion intended was that the basket was empty. It was then surrounded by a few bamboos, and round the bamboos was wound a slip of dirty cotton cloth, jargon going on vigorously all the time: one man responding to the other's jargon. In a few minutes the bamboos and basket were kicked over, all empty, and the woman forced herself, from the outside, through the circle of servants and others who were looking on, and presented herself before us at the steps of the portico. I am aware that all this is done by Lynn, and Maskelyne and

Cooke and others, but they perform on a stage, with their audience in front of them, nobody at the back. Here the trick was done under a bright sun, in the middle of the day, on the gravel just under our eyes, with servants and strangers surrounding it, by men who had no mechanical appliances, and, being nearly naked, could not possibly conceal any apparatus about their persons. The same set of men performed before the Prince of Wales, and an account appeared in the newspapers of these very tricks, but I thought you would like to hear from me what I saw myself with my own eyes. Then there was a man with two little birds on his finger. He stationed a boy about thirty feet off, and stuck a little ring in the boy's nose; at the word of command one of the birds flew from the man's finger right at the boy's nose, seized the ring, and brought it back to the man. He then tossed up a little red fluffy tassel into the air; the bird flew at it, seized it in the air, and brought it back to him.

Here, at Ootacamund, we have got back suddenly into old England again. I mean, so far as hoar frost, blankets and fires are concerned. My bath of a morning and the landscape from the window remind me of Craven Cottage before we go out hunting. They even have hunting here, but not till the season, which begins in March—a regular pack of foxhounds, meets, and all correct, but instead of the fox they hunt the jackal. It must be break-neck work up and down these hills, which now are as hard as brickbats; perhaps in March, when the rain has fallen, the surface may be softer. I really have not seen a horse or even a pony in India which I would care to possess; the horses are either second-rate, shuffling Arabs, about 14 hands high, or coarse Cape or Australian importations without action, which would discredit an omnibus in London. The ponies come chiefly from Burmah, and are called Pegu ponies, not quite

13 hands, rough and without action, but wiry, and able to do a day's work. We have been riding them on these hills, and find them safe over rough roads, and lasting. There is still good sport to be had in these wild Nielgherry Hills, if a man knows how to set about it. About eight or ten miles off, in various directions, are travellers' bungalows, empty houses, with one attendant living in each, where a sportsman, bringing all his own food and things, can put up for a week or more, and make that place the base of his operations. Here, with native beaters got together on the spot, he can beat the jungles round about, and can generally fall in with a sambur, antelope, bear, or sometimes with a tiger or leopard or cheetah. It is an enormous extent of wild country, but that in the plains towards Mysore is still more vast; only in the plains fever is rife, and sport cannot be carried on there without risk to health. Perhaps our brace of grouse at Dolly, with health and old England about us, is the best, after all. For a traveller there is great excitement and novelty in this country, but as a resident I should not care for it; the climate would not suit me all the year round—it is not bracing enough. In these hills there is an exhilarating breeze morning and evening, like our autumns in England. But below, in the plains, the atmosphere, if not actually sultry, is vapid, and devoid of freshness at the best. There is no inducement to take exercise, but, on the contrary, every temptation to remain idle in your cane armchair and literally to do nothing.

There are three distinct aboriginal tribes in the Nielgherries—the Todas, about 600 in number, who claim to be lords of the soil, and to whom a certain class of the poorer cultivators pay a small tribute in kind—our Government to a certain extent also acknowledge the claim, and allow them rights of pasturage over the waste lands; secondly, the Corrumbas, about the same in number, but a very inferior race

GROUPE of TODAS, or
Aborigines of the Nielgherries

Sketched from life at Martimund. 17 Dec. '6

p. 90.

to the Todas—they live on roots and in holes of the rocks, are short in stature, a kind of Earthmen, and are very rarely seen in any civilized neighbourhood; and thirdly, the Kotas, who number about 300 only. All these tribes are gradually diminishing in number owing to intermarriage amongst themselves. I came across a family of Todas. Very black they were, with a large quantity of thick, black hair, growing low down on the forehead, but not ungainly either in face or figure, somewhat an exaggerated type of our gipsies. They had their small herd of buffaloes and tract of grazing ground round their huts, but nevertheless pursued us, begging.

TRICHINOPOLY,
Sunday, 24th December, 1876.

I AM housed (if I may use an Irishism) here in a tent in the collector's garden. Mr. Webster, the judge, who was to have taken us in, has gone to Madras, and therefore transferred us to Mr. Sewell, the collector, and he very kindly put up a tent for me, as his house could not accommodate all. At 1.30 a.m. this morning I was awake and fidgeting about the tent, for the musquitoes had got seisin of me, when I heard the patter of the first large drops of rain on the roof of the tent. "Oh, what a blessing!" thought I, "to this famine-stricken country." We had not had a drop of rain ourselves since leaving the Mediterranean, two months and more ago; and here, in South India, everything was perishing for want of it. No such famine had occurred within the memory of man, and all idea of rain at this season had been abandoned. "A few heat drops," I said to myself; but no, the patter continued and increased till at last it settled down to heavy tropical rain. I turned into bed again, experiencing a new sensation as if I was sleeping under a large umbrella. I awoke again at five, and found that the tent ropes had slackened, the tent pegs had become loose, and my roof had bulged in, and it was drip, drip, in all directions. However, I was only too glad that the heavy rain had continued all night. Whilst I was moving my bed away from the drip, in the dark, and shifting some of my clothes from this quality of mercy, smack went some of the tent pegs, and a good portion of the tent collapsed, carrying away some of the crockery with it, with a bang. I summoned the servants, who fortunately were within earshot, and they got more help, and we had things righted; but Rama said to me, "Master, go inside; if it come wet sometimes tent fall down altogether." It was clear I had not yet seen the shady side of tent life. A large quantity of rain has fallen already, and if it goes on in this way some of the crops will be saved; the tanks will be filled, herbage spring up, and the wretched cattle (now going about like skeletons) will find food. It is indeed an opportune visitation. The descent of the Ghaut, on returning from the Nielgherries, impressed me as much as the ascent did. I never saw so striking a scene. Imagine an Alpine pass of the first magnitude with the addition of tropical vegetation of the most varied character at the base. That night we slept at Erode, at the station, for there are very few inns in this country. I occupied a double-bedded room jointly with a stranger. I asked the woman of the station who he was, as I had misgivings about the rupees I carried with me in my pockets. "A very nice man," she said; "there he is!" pointing to a rough hairy man, smoking on the platform. He turned out to be inspector of points and crossings on the railway—a good sort of rough Scotchman; but he snored terrifically. At Tanjore, our next halt, we were most hospitably received by Mr. Thomas, the collector. It shows how easily false impressions may be formed of a man one does not know personally. He had lost his wife recently by cholera, and had taken up, we were told, Lord Radstock's views of religion. On that account we changed our programme so that we might go to Trichinopoly first, and spend Sunday and Christmas Day here, and not at Tanjore. He turned out, on acquaintance, to be a most cheery fellow, like poor John Reynolds in face, liveliness and manner, full of jokes, and a great sportsman. It was quite a relief to me to talk to him about horses, shooting and fishing. He has published an excellent book on Indian fish. He again wished me to stay behind with him, promising me black buck, snipe and sport of all kinds, but time would not admit of it. Tanjore is famous for its grand pagoda. It certainly is a noble specimen of Hindoo art. I do not myself care for Hindoo art. It is full of grotesque deformities, which recommend themselves only to men, like Monier, skilled in Hindoo mythology; but to me, Siva with his six or eight arms, riding on a deformed bull, or Vishnu on some other beast or bird, equally out of drawing, are alike monstrous, inartistic and absurd. The whole paraphernalia, however, of Brahmins, attendants, ceremonies, groups, colours, taken in conjunction with the Eastern architecture, interests me from its character and novelty, and so I enjoy it as much as Monier does. We are always met on these occasions with great respect and courtesy by the priests and attendants, and garlanded with masses of oleanders as we go away. What interested me still more was a visit of ceremony we paid to the Ranees of Tanjore at the Palace. The Rajah of Tanjore has left no son—only a daughter, the present Princess of Tanjore, who has gone up to Delhi for the great assemblage there, and twelve widows, who are the Ranees, and live in the Palace. The Princess is married, but has no child—consequently the Ranees, more to spite the Princess (for they fight like mothers-in-law and children in our own country) than for any other reason, wish to adopt a son. They cannot do so without the consent of our Government, and they desired to have a conference with Mr. Thomas, who, as collector, is supreme at Tanjore, to talk over the matter. Mr. Thomas took us with him to the Palace. We were received at the entrance, in Eastern fashion, by a bevy of turbaned and bedizened fellows, who constitute the idle hangers on at all palaces, and conducted to the hall or large room where the Ranees had enshrined themselves, for they were not visible—a striped curtain shut off a portion of the room. In the curtain, parallel with the ground and about two feet from it, was a band of net-work about four inches wide, so that the

Ranees, squatted on the ground on the other side, could peep through the net-work at us and we could not see them. We were seated round the table close to the curtain, and at one end of the table sat the adopted son, dressed in white, with a cap of gold, a wretched looking Jewish kind of creature, as yellow as his cap, with nails an inch long and as nervous and uncomfortable as possible. Behind us—some seated, some standing—were all the tag-rag and bob-tail of the Palace, something like the chorus of warriors and nobles at 1*s.* a night when Otello is performed at the Royal Italian Opera. The conversation was carried on briskly in Tamil between Mr. Thomas and the Ranees, who seemed to hold their own all the better for being behind the curtain. It turned on the terms on which the British Government would sanction the adoption. That over, I said to Mr. Thomas, in joke, "Tell the ladies that we have come all the way from England on purpose to see them, and ask them to come out from behind the curtain and show themselves." The chief voice amongst them at once replied, "In the face of our adopted son before you, you see our faces; you must be content." An excellent answer, and we were accordingly obliged to be satisfied with the yellow, narrow-chested creature seated at the table before us. Nothing shows our moral power in the East more than an audience of this kind. Here we were, five of us, English—that is, Thomas, the sub-collector, and our three selves—in shooting coats, in the precincts of the Palace of one of the oldest dynasties in Southern India, surrounded by all the pomp and circumstance of the Palace, and yet recognized as the paramount lords of all. Nothing can be done, from the adoption of a son down to the purchase of a carriage horse, without our consent. How is this? There are no troops within 100 miles. Thomas, his two assistants, the doctor and a missionary parson are the only Englishmen in the place, and yet we hold all the power. The firmness and integrity of our character and the natural distrust and weakness of the native character, supply the answer. We were all again garlanded with oleanders on our exit from the Palace. Before leaving, the court fool, or jester, came forward and complained to Mr. Thomas that his pay of six rupees a month had been stopped. Monier says it is only in the very old courts that this personage is kept going, and I suppose he is now doomed at Tanjore—poor fool! Another interesting and thoroughly Indian scene was enacted before us at Tanjore—namely, a Nautch. It was held at 8 o'clock at night, in the porte cochère of Mr. Thomas's house, which formed a natural kind of theatre, as steps led up from it to the house. We all sat on chairs placed on the top step, and below, on the carpeted ground, the performance took place. No scene-painter was necessary. The magnificent aruns, bigonias and calladiums at the back and sides of the portico formed appropriate scenery, all lighted up with as many duplex and other lamps and candles as Thomas's butler could stick on the steps of the portico. There were five girls and a number of native musicians and attendants. The girls were dressed in sparkling bodices, with gold-tissue skirts gathered up between the legs and falling full in front, brilliant satin trousers, and covered with real jewellery; head, neck, ears, nose and fingers were a mass of gold and precious stones. They danced set figures in Oriental fashion with great precision and effect, and good time was kept by bells fastened round their ankles. The dances over, we descended the steps of the portico and examined the girls and their jewellery. The jewels bore the examination better than the girls. Apart from their ornaments they would not pass muster; but the jewels were lovely and so Eastern. I longed to pocket them. The value of each girl's jewels was stated to be 700*l*. or 800*l*. Before they left, two or three of the girls came forward, and, in serious language, complained to Mr. Thomas of the article in the Penal Code, which prevents women of this character from bringing up their daughters as courtesans. They look on it as a profession, a legitimate and hereditary profession, in which they are entitled to educate their daughters. To judge from their jewels, it must be a paying one. It was another proof, added to the scene at the Palace and the appeal from the jester, of the power which the English collector is supposed to possess. The people think he can do anything.

Christmas Day. How different to the same in England! thermometer 82°, but a drizzling rain off and on all day. My quarters were shifted last night from the tent to the house owing to the rain—half eaten up by musquitoes. Drove before breakfast to the Great Temple at Seringham, three miles off, an aggregation of gopuras, or entrance gates, colonnaded halls and pagodas, all enclosed by walled-in enclosures, one within the other, the outer quadrangle being a quarter of a mile square. Within are native huts, where dwell those who have retired in their old age to these sacred precincts. We were received with great courtesy by the custodians, and the magnificent jewels of the idol were exhibited to us, displayed on a table, and said to be worth £70,000 or £80,000. Thence to Jemba Keshwara, another large block of gopuras, colonnaded halls and pagodas, similar to Seringham and almost equally striking. Were garlanded with oleanders at each place. The wonderful Rock of Trichinopoly rises abruptly to a height of 400 feet from the town below, and looks like a pile of great water-worn boulders of stone, one above the other, crowned with a temple; the access to the top being by long flights of steps, partly artificial and partly hewn out of the rock. From the top there is an extensive panoramic view over the plains, the two rivers, Cauvery and Coloroon, bounded by the distant mountains towards the north. The whole of the rock was illuminated on the occasion of the Prince of Wales' visit.

TRICHINOPOLY,
December 26th, 1876.

ENGLISH newspapers reach us in India a day after the fair, and the appetite for home news is consequently dulled by the interval which has necessarily elapsed after the event. I have, however, been much struck with an observation in the Premier's speech at the Mansion House dinner (with reference to European politics), that ours was a rule of sympathy and not of force, as applicable to India. Old residents in the country may tell us that there is a growing want of sympathy between the native population in India and their English rulers. Perhaps remarks to that effect may just now be made with more bitterness than sincerity, owing to the irritation caused amongst civilians in India by three well-known cases:—first, where a civilian was directly rebuked for his supposed harsh treatment of a native at a public assemblage during the Prince of Wales' visit last year; —secondly, by the instance known as "Fuller's Case," which called forth Lord Lytton's celebrated minute, and more recently by the "Weld Case," where a civilian has been suspended for a supposed indignity offered to the natives, by exhuming the body of a holy man which had been buried too near a well, the water of which was in use in the neighbourhood. A good deal of excitement prevails in India from the discussion of these cases, and a certain amount of antagonism between the two races at the present moment, but only temporary it may be hoped, is the natural result of the discussion.

Apart from feeling and prejudice I offer my impressions, as a tourist, that our rule in India, if not a rule of sympathy, is at least a rule of justice. There are, of course, many separate branches of administration in the public service in India, but I will adduce the duties of a collector by way of illustration. All three Presidencies are divided into collectorates, each collectorate being presided over by a collector, with a sub-collector, magistrates, and staff of officers under him, totally distinct from the judge and judicial staff in the same division. The primary duty of a collector was formerly to get in the land revenue of the territory within his jurisdiction, and hence the name. He has, however, much more than that to do now; in fact, the collection of the revenue forms the least important part of his duties. A more appropriate name for him would be administrator of the district, every department of which, except the judicial, is under his control. He is responsible for the peace of the district; he has to look after the roads and public buildings, the proper supply of water, the repair of tanks, bridges, and embankments, the sanitary condition of the people; he establishes dispensaries, and visits prisons; he plants and improves, and advises with the municipality, where there is one, and, where there is none, himself decides on the appropriation of local funds for all or any of those special objects. He sits as a magistrate, takes original charges, and hears appeals from the magistrates and officers under him.

The better to enable him to become acquainted with the wants of every part of his district and to afford the people greater facility for representing their grievances, as well as to collect the tribute, he moves about his district in tents for eight or nine months of each year, pitching his tents in the neighbourhood of different villages, so that he may himself judge of local requirements and that the outlying inhabitants may have personal access to him. In short, the general welfare of the district is committed to his care and he has to provide for it.

Driving out the other day with a collector in the Madras Presidency, whose guest I was at his head-quarters, I observed a concourse of persons assembled in his garden. I asked who those people were. He replied, "They are petitioners, all of whom have or fancy they have some grievance to be redressed." I said, "I suppose you have stated days for hearing these cases?"—"Oh, no," he replied, "Every day of the week; fifty or sixty people come to me every day with specific complaints." I was with him one afternoon whilst he disposed of these cases. They comprised every sort of grievance connected with land tenure, magisterial work, and charitable relief. He sat in an armchair under the verandah of his house, with his civil clerk, his magisterial clerk, and a couple of policemen on his right, and two or three peons, or office messengers, on his left. A list had been previously made of all the complainants present and a précis of such complaints as had been submitted in writing. The number of persons present on the occasion to which I allude was sixty. As the name was called out in order, the man or woman advanced to the foot of the collector's chair and stated his or her grievance. It was listened to with patience and determined on the spot, with explanations or advice given in the vernacular, my friend being as conversant with Tamil as with English. It was a domestic tribunal, intelligible and apparently satisfactory to all concerned, and very interesting it was to witness these half-clothed natives come forward, one by one, with their obeisance, state their case directly and personally and submit willingly to the decision.

Take another illustration, namely, the assessment of the land tax. In Bombay, if not in the other Presidencies, the settlement of the tax lasts for thirty years, when there is a careful revision of the assessment. For that purpose the officers of the Government communicate directly with the ryots, the lands are classified according to their physical or mechanical composition, and the outcome of the produce, per acre, is converted into a money equivalent on a fair basis. The returns made by the local officers are sent up to the chief revenue officer of the Presidency, who submits them to the collector of the district for his remarks, and the tax is not imposed until it has obtained the ultimate sanction of the Government. When it is considered that British India contains nearly a million square miles, paying revenue to the Viceroy, the amount of labour involved in the assessment will be appreciated.

I have reason to believe that the judicial, educational, postal, and other departments of the service, are administered by our upright, independent and efficient British public servants in India with the same care and the same scrupulous regard to the interests of the native population. I should add, also, that the posts of all the sub-revenue officials and magistrates, as well as of the district judges, and the staff in both cases, are occupied by natives.

I have yet another special illustration to adduce, and will not then further trespass on your patience. The inhabitants of the British Isles, and especially of the Principality, do not know what it is to suffer from want of rain. Here, in Southern India, the rainfall this season has not been one-fourth of the average, and the consequence is that the crops have failed and famine is sore in the land. About 15,000,000 people are affected by the famine, and this is only the commencement of the evil. Soon will follow a famine of water, against which there is no relief. Infant children will be the first to die, and will be swept off wholesale; the cattle also must perish. The Government are acting with energy, and are establishing relief works in numerous localities throughout the Presidency; but if no rain should fall in the meantime, they have four months of growing destitution and misery before them, and plenty of anxious work to be done.

The foregoing instances afford, I think reasonable, grounds for the conclusion at which I have arrived, that our rule in India is a rule, if not of sympathy, at least of justice.

RAMNAD,

Saturday, 30th December, 1876.

WE have got into an out-of-the-way corner of India here, have had a good deal of trouble and fatigue to get here, and shall have more before we can get out of it; but we had time on our hands, and the question was how best to use it. The coasting steamers from Bombay touch at Tuticorin once a week only for Colombo, namely, on Sundays. To-morrow would have been too soon for us, and we had therefore a week in hand till the following Sunday. The great temple at Ramiseram, at the extreme southern point of the island of Paumben, is the object of pilgrimage with thousands of Hindoos; and as Temple lore was Monier's chief object in his visit to the south, we resolved to make a pilgrimage there too. But if it adds to the merit of the pilgrimage to go through much trouble and fatigue about it, we and all other pilgrims to Ramiseram ought to be well thought of for our pains. Six hours of railway through an interesting country, bounded by blue hills in all directions, with a cloudy atmosphere and unusual freedom from dust, took us from Trichinopoly to Madura last Tuesday, the 26th. At Madura we were received by Mr. Hutchins, the judge there, and his wife, and comfortably accommodated in his spacious bungalow. You may imagine the area of ground on which it stands when I tell you that the verandahs on each side of it, supported by heavy chunam columns, round which were twined brilliant Bougainvillia and blue convolvulus creepers, were 90 yards in length. The couple have no children, and interest themselves in the house and garden. Mr. Hutchins is especially nursing a banyan tree in the garden, which already measures 180 yards in circumference. This tree (as you know) throws down pendant shoots, which take root and form in time a forest of trunks. By encouraging some of these shoots and pruning others the colonnade of trunks can be made very effective, and some years hence I have no doubt this tree will be a wonder. The great Pagoda at Madura is the sight of the place, more ornate, with richer carving than even that at Seringham, and there we saw Hindooism rampant. A festival was going on—three elephants in procession, preceded by Nautch girls, musicians and priests, and followed by a large crowd. Monier has always much attention paid to him by the Brahmins on these occasions, and we are garlanded with oleanders and brought to the front in order that we may see everything. It is a nice, clean, open town in itself,—boulevards of palmyras and cocoa-nut trees, the natives, their huts and habits, being more in accordance with African scenes than Indian. To leave the rail and plunge into village wheel tracks, with a view to the Ramiseram expedition, a good deal of organization was necessary. A regular transit had to be arranged in bullock bandies for the 70 miles from Madura to Ramnad; a bullock bandy is a common tilted two-wheeled cart of the country, drawn by a couple of Brahminy bullocks yoked curricle-fashion. For night journeys the bandy is planked over, and a mattrass laid on the planks, so that the traveller can sleep at full length on the mattrass, if the road is pretty even. Two of these were engaged for us, one a wide one for Monier and Stanley, the other for myself. Mrs. Hutchins kindly put up for us a basket of provisions—very necessary—and leaving our heavy luggage and one of our servants at Madura, we started on our journey at 6 o'clock in the evening of the 28th. It was moonlight; but the cover of the bandy is not favourable to view. However, I could see that we twice crossed the dry sandy bed of the River Vaigay, and felt, as well as saw, that we were launched on country tracks, not roads. After nine or ten hours of bumping and thumping I could see the leading bandy brought up, and the men busy about it with a lantern—the axle had broken—Stanley's weight had proved too much for native iron. Luckily we were only a mile from the village where we were to halt and breakfast, and the broken trap was dragged to that point and there left. Whilst we were at breakfast on Mrs. Hutchins' basket at the Travellers' bungalow at 6 in the morning, a village cart was requisitioned, into which our servant and the luggage were transferred. Monier and Stanley got into my bandy, the mattrass being removed and replaced with seats, and we started afresh for Ramnad, 23 miles; but such roads, the like of it was never seen in Europe,—only tracks, constantly shifting, over sand and open land. I walked a good bit of the way as a choice of two evils, and after eight hours consumed in doing the 23 miles, we reached Ramnad at 3.30 yesterday afternoon. I was so sorry for the poor little Brahminy bullocks, which are the universal beasts of draught in this country. It is a small animal, not much bigger than a good-sized calf in England; the heavy yoke rests on its neck just in front of the hump; there is no other harness, and it drags by the pressure of the yoke against the hump, the driver sitting on the pole by way of adding to the weight of the yoke on the neck. Of course we had several changes on the road; but it was surprising how well these patient little creatures did their work, now and then on even ground breaking out into a jog-trot, and never leaving the clumsy heavy vehicle in a hole or refusing to pull, though the neck was often badly galled. We are the guests of Mr. Lee Warner here, but he only arrived here from England two days ago, and consequently we have to rough it, as he has nothing in order. I had fortunately brought towel and soap, and we all had our resais and pillows, otherwise we should have been badly off.

We start to-night in country bandies for Paumben, 23 or 24 miles of sandy road, and I will go on with my letter when the journey has been accomplished.

Island of Paumben, Sunday, 31st Dec. We have had another long night journey over village tracks in bullock bandies, and arrived here safely at 6 this morning. At all events, we have now seen how our forefathers travelled in India before the days of railways. It has been a singular experience. When our plans had been settled at Ramnad, the native assistant was commissioned to engage four bandies; one for each of ourselves, and the fourth for Rama and the Madura peon, who had accompanied us all the way, and our luggage, to start from Ramnad at 6 p.m. At least three hours before that time the bandies had been dropping in, in the compound of Lee Warner's house. It was so primitive, these clumsy two-wheeled carts covered with a tilt of rough matting, with the pair of Brahminy bullocks belonging to each lying down by the side of the cart, chewing the cud, their gentle expression and soft eyes as much as saying, "We are ready to start now, or will wait six or twelve hours, or any time, when you will." At 6 p.m., however, a mattrass had been put into each cart, over a layer of hay (none of the carts had springs), and our preparations were completed, and off we went in solemn procession. When night closed and the moon got up, it did look so weird,—the line of carts with the white bullocks, and black drivers enveloped in white to keep out the night air, passing in silence over the wide expanse of sand interspersed with palmyra trees, and along the margin now and then of a gloomy lagoon, no sound being heard but the croak of a frog and the tinkle of the bullock bells. I could not sleep, nor could Monier, for though the track was across loose sand, the thumps and jolts of the clumsy vehicle shook us to pieces. Whilst I was peering out of my tilt a ghostly figure passed by at full trot; it was the dawk or Tapaul runner with the mail bag balanced on the top of his head, and a stick in his hand with rings on it, jingling as he ran. He did not look to the right or left, but passed between us and the edge of the desolate lagoon with no noise but the jingle of the rings. Poor fellow, I thought to myself, he must have a desolate run of it every night. Jog, jog, thump, jolt all night, our carts crawled over the sandy waste at two miles an hour, and turned us out at Mundepam, the margin of the channel which separates the Island of Paumben from the mainland, at 5 a.m. Here, by moonlight, we had to transfer ourselves and baggage into an open country boat to cross the channel. A few naked men, their black skins glancing under the moon, helped us; the bandies were paid off, the great cotton sail was hoisted, and we ran across the channel in good style. The boat was beached on the sandy shore of the island, away from any habitation, and we landed on the sand as if we had been the first discoverers of Paumben. Rama, the servant, lit a fire under some scrub, and we had some hot tea out of his kettle; and whilst the peon was sent inland to see if he could find help, I walked and had a delicious bath in the sea. By-and-by the natives came down with a pony for Monier, who was done up with the two night journeys, and we were conducted to a rough kind of bungalow occupied temporarily by Mr. Turner, an assistant-collector of Ramnad. He and his young wife had been expecting us, and had put up two tents for us on the sand close to the house, one for Monier and Stanley, the other for me. Monier was unequal to any further exertion, and retired to his tent for the rest of the day. I cannot account for the difference between him and me in that respect, but I do not feel fatigue; and therefore after 10 o'clock breakfast I hired a pony, and rode to the

Great Temple of Ramiseram, eight miles on the opposite shore of the island. It is, no doubt, a grand pile of building, the more wonderful from its position at this very remote end of the world. Two of the corridors, which enclosed the Pagoda, are 240 yards in length. I paced them, and the perspective views of the carved and painted pillars the whole of this length is striking, but I had already seen the Pagodas of Seringham and Madura and Tanjore, and found nothing exceptionally fine in Ramiseram. It is, however, more sacred than any of them, and the poor zealous Hindoo devotees flock there in thousands from all parts of India, the temple Brahmins, of course, reaping a rich harvest in some form or other from all this enthusiasm, which they take care to foment. Mr. Turner told us that not long since a father and son had walked the whole way from Cashmere to Ramiseram—2,000 miles or more—on a pilgrimage to the Temple, carrying with them a pot of Ganges water to pour over the god on arriving at the temple. On the very day of their arrival at Ramiseram the father died of cholera, without having been able to pour the Ganges water over the god. The son, a child of ten years of age, was left a complete stranger in the place, and unable to speak a word of the language. He was anxious to fulfil the object of the long and weary pilgrimage, and to pour the Ganges water over the god, but the Brahmins required him first to pay the customary fee, a few annas only. He had no money whatever, and the Brahmins consequently refused permission. This came to the ears of the deputy-collector, who at once went to the temple, and under his protection the boy poured the Ganges water over the god. Mr. Turner himself then took charge of the boy, and placed him at the High School at Ramnad, where he now is. I myself saw more than one pilgrim carrying pots of Ganges water for the same purpose.

A couple of pots are generally carried, suspended from the two ends of a bamboo slung across the shoulders. On my way back from the temple I fortunately met Mr. and Mrs. Turner and some ladies, who are at Paumben on a visit, going to evening church. I am ashamed to say I had forgotten it was Sunday. I handed my pony over to a servant, and was glad to be able to accompany them,—such a primitive service in a small missionary church. The bell was tolled by a naked black boy, the bell itself being hung on a tree just outside the door. The service was performed by a native ordained clergyman from Tinnevelly, and the congregation consisted of Mr. Turner's party, two or three other English, and half a dozen blacks. The text, "There was no room for them in the inn." It was the only service during the day, and it was good for me to be there.

TINNEVELLY,
4th January, 1877.

I POSTED a letter to you yesterday morning only, on our arrival by sea at Tuticorin; but it strikes me if I do not write again before crossing to Ceylon, that you may not hear from me for an indefinite time. I therefore intend to post this on our return to Tuticorin on Sunday, before we embark for Colombo, so that it will travel by rail viâ Bombay. I was in such a hurry to save the mail yesterday morning that I did not tell you about our voyage from Paumben to Tuticorin in the wretched country craft we chartered in Paumben channel. It was a great deep tub of a thing, the planks of all shapes and sizes, and worm-eaten; the spars unshaped, too, and broken and spliced with thin rope made of cocoa-nut fibre; cotton sails all falling to pieces; a few planks aft covering over a hole which might be called a cabin; all the rest of the tub a deep, open well. We had laid in a stock of provisions; a couple of live fowls—one of them turned out a precious old one,—a dozen eggs, some curry condiments, bread, a tin of soup, &c.; but how to cook? that was the question. Well, the old rusty anchor was weighed by the eight naked black men and two naked boys, all Mahommedans, calling out to each other in wild responses as they tugged at the rough cocoa-nut fibre cable; the old ragged jib was set, and we rounded to the strong north-east wind, and then hoisted our other tattered sails, and the old tub began to swish, swish through the water with half a gale of wind fortunately directly behind her. It is astonishing how soon one adapts oneself to circumstances. I had conjured up all manner of horrors. These savages, I thought to myself, have no compass. Suppose we are driven out to sea. We have only three chatty pots of water on board, and here we are twelve men on board. Suppose one of those chatty pots is broken—why the supply of fresh water would not last us a day. Suppose these fellows combine and cut our throats; or a mast breaks and we lie like a log on the sea. Suppose a hundred things quite within the range of possibility. But when the old rickety concern once felt the influence of the wind and began to "speak," I forgot these imaginary horrors; more especially when Rama (our servant) inquired when we would like tiffin. "Tiffin?" I said, "all very well; but how are you to cook it?" There was a thick layer of sand at the bottom of the vessel, and three stones. Rama said, "I cook here;" so he took off his coat, put the stones together on the sand, and by collecting some pieces of wood, and rigging out a shelter, he got up a decent fire on the sand between the stones. I soon became interested in the operations, and sat with my legs dangling on a plank looking down into the well. One of the two chickens was soon slaughtered, poor thing! and plucked; a small clay pot was found for boiling the rice; one of the two black boys was set to work to pound the curry stuff; and in due course Rama turned us out a capital chicken-curry; that is to say, the whole was put and mixed in another small clay pot, and we three ate it out of the pot, turn and turn about. Then, as we passed some sacred spot in the distant shore one of the crew stood up, and placing his hands in position recited some kind of litany, the rest of the crew joining melodiously in the refrain. At 7 p.m. we ran under the lee of a promontory and anchored. Rama again turned to, to cook on the three stones, and produced chicken No. 2 boiled, preceded by the soup for dinner with potatoes. In the meantime, the crew had boiled a large chatty pot of rice with fish curry, for their own dinner, all of which proved very amusing to me, seated on my plank looking down on them. It was a magnificent starlight night; the uncouth boat, the naked crew, the unknown shore with the glare here and there of a fire burning on the beach, gave the scene the charm of novelty, and it needed that to compensate us for the hole abaft in which we laid down for the night. At midnight the crew were again astir weighing anchor; but the wind having dropped, we rolled about on the swell, until the dawn enabled me to emerge and view the glories of an Eastern sunrise on the ocean. By 8 a.m. we were off the sparkling little town of Tuticorin, landed (not sorry to be out of our old tub), and remained there all yesterday at the Travellers' bungalow. There was a great deal of life on the shore, which boasts of a small pier and a good broad esplanade. The roadstead was full of ships bringing rice for the famine and exporting coolies to Ceylon. The exodus of coolies answers both purposes—it relieves the famine districts in Southern India from a surplus population, and furnishes labour to the coffee cultivators in Ceylon. 300,000 coolies pass to and from Ceylon annually on an average—more, of course, this famine year; the trading schooners carry them across at two rupees ahead; the Ceylon planters are glad to get them as coffee-pickers. We left Tuticorin to-day at 11 a.m. for this place, arriving here at 3 p.m., and are housed at Mr. Carr's, the Judge.

Friday, 5th Jan. Mr. and Mrs. Carr arrived from the Assimboo Hills this morning. Tinnevelly, being systematically irrigated from the River Tamra Purnee, is surrounded by luxuriant crops and rich foliage; the bright grateful green of the rice fields stands out in refreshing contrast from the miles and miles of dry, hot, barren sand which are traversed after leaving Tuticorin. The Carrs have carried the system of irrigation into their own garden and they rejoice in a regular English lawn (the only one I have yet seen), and in lovely flowers of all kinds. In and out of the house everything seems fresh and in apple-pie order; English comforts combined with tropical beauties; a large swimming-bath, for instance, in which Mr. Carr and I have been disporting ourselves this morning,—indeed, it is the only house I have been to in India which looks like a home. On every other house is written in unmistakeable characters—"This is not our resting-place." The occupants all have old England in view,—India is no abiding city for them. Even Mr. Carr said to me to-day, "Don't talk to me of England; I make myself happy here. I try to do so at least; I do the best I can, but I can't bear to think of England." Such is the feeling with every Englishman I have yet come across. I don't wonder at it. I declare for the old country. Grumblers and valetudinarians be satisfied with it,—there is no country in the world, be assured, like England. Tuticorin and Tinnevelly are the only places which I have seen where there are marked evidences of the progress of Christianity. Here there is a large compound enclosing Dr. Serjeant's house, schools, and domiciles for fifty native boys and as many girls, and a spacious church. Dr. Caldwell and Dr. Serjeant are the two missionary bishops in embryo. Both unluckily are absent; but we saw Mrs. Serjeant yesterday (unexpected by her) in the large back verandah at her house, surrounded by her girls. They were fifty-two in number, all dressed alike in short scarlet bodices and a neat pink-check cloth wound round the body and thrown over the shoulder. Their hair parted in the middle and tied neatly in a knot at the back,—all with earrings and some with nose rings. They stood in rows and sang "Safe in the arms of Jesus," and two other hymns in English, and also some hymns in Tamil, taking parts and with great harmony. Two of the girls read to us afterwards in English,—it was an impressive scene. Afterwards we drove to the girls' school, under the presidency of the Reverend Mr. Lash and Mrs. Lash. About seventy girls, all native converts of the higher castes, are boarded and lodged in the compound and trained for school teachers. Schools have been established by Mr. Lash in various neighbouring villages, and the girls, after they are certificated, are sent out as superintendents of these village schools. Mr. Lash said he had about 1,200 children altogether in these village schools. It is not a condition that the children should be Christians, but a Christian catechism is taught and Scripture stories read in all the schools, the parents never objecting. Constant application is made to him for the establishment of these schools. The church, a plain spacious airy building, can hold 1,000 persons. Every Sunday between 600 and 700 native converts are present, the services being conducted in Tamil by native ordained ministers. The number of communicants on Sundays exceeds 100 on the average. Mr. Carr told us that there is an instance of a whole village having gone over bodily to Christianity, and handed over their village pagoda to the missionaries. Christianity is an undoubted fact here. So is the Roman form of it at Tuticorin, where there are two large Roman Catholic churches, one of them nearly 100 years old. That church has been purposely so contrived as to be only one step in advance of the Hindoo pagoda. The images at the altar are periodically painted and dressed very much as the Hindoo god in his holy of holies is painted and dressed; Christian symbols are placed and enshrined exactly after the fashion of Hindoo symbols; processions are arranged like the Hindoo processions; between the massive buttresses outside the church stands the car on which the Virgin is seated and drawn, the facsimile of the car of Vishnu or Siva outside the Hindoo temple; lights, bells, flowers, tinfoil, perfume, are the accompaniments of both. The Hindoo passes on to Christianity in that way by very easy stages, and finds himself transferred from one atmosphere of symbols into another much of the same character. The result is, that at Tuticorin, out of a total population of 12,000, 6,000 are said to be Roman Catholics. These are remarkable facts, and I think the leaven is leavening the whole lump, or will do so here in Southern India in time. I was out this morning before breakfast sketching by myself. Of course a large, orderly, curious crowd formed round me. After I had finished I asked, "Which of you can speak English?" One man replied, "I can." I asked, "What are you?" he said, "Employed on the railway." I inquired, "Hindoo or Christian?" he said "Christian." Another man, squatted close by my side, pointing to my sketch-book, said, "Please, let me see your other performances." I turned over the leaves of the book and explained the sketches. He said, "I am fond of art." When I got up to go home he followed me and asked questions about art, light and shade, colour, &c. He had nothing on but a loin cloth. I inquired, "Are you a Christian?" "No," he said, "I am a Brahmin. But," he added, "there is very little difference. I believe in one Supreme God, and I agree with the moral precepts of Jesus Christ, but I deny his Deity." Whether they will eventually become Christians or not, en masse, it is impossible to predict, but the educated Hindoos certainly hold very advanced opinions on religion, and look on idols as symbols only. With regard to actual conversions to Christianity at the present time, I ought to have mentioned that the number of converts in the Tinnevelly district exceeds 60,000 Protestants, and about the same number of Roman Catholics. The steamer for Colombo will be in Tuticorin Roads at midnight to-night. We embark at 7 o'clock to-morrow morning, and sail for Colombo at noon to-morrow.

Colombo, Ceylon, 8th January. We left Tuticorin yesterday morning in a sailing-boat, having to sail out 6 or 7 miles to the "Arabia," the British India Steam Company's steamer, which was anchored in the roadstead. She had arrived punctually during the night, but, owing to shoal water, could not come nearer in. We and two others were the only passengers; each, therefore, had a cabin to himself. We found her a clean vessel, with an excellent cuisine. She discharged 2,500 bags of rice in boats for the famine districts, and took in 3 lacs of rupees in bullion, conveyed out to her in the same boat that took us. Each box of bullion (there must have been fifty boxes at least) had a piece of bamboo tied to it at the end of 15 or 20 yards of rope, so that in case our boat had capsized or a box had tumbled overboard the piece of bamboo would have acted as a buoy. The "Arabia" weighed anchor at noon, and after a pleasant voyage arrived at Colombo at 7 o'clock this morning; distance 150 miles from Tuticorin. I need not say that here, in Colombo, everything is associated in my thoughts with Willy and the Andersons—Government House, the racecourse, grand stand, Galle Face Drive, all recall to me the life which they lived here long ago. I can now realize it all. I have been to-day to Government House, and have been introduced to Sir William Gregory, the Governor. What a fine spacious house it is! What royal entertaining rooms! We are lodged at the Galle Face Hotel—bad is the best—its only recommendation is that the roar of the sea is close under my ground-floor bed-room window. Equatorial heat even at this season!

KANDY, CEYLON,
Sunday, 14th January, 1877.

I WAS on the deck of the "Arabia" at 5.30 a.m., as she approached Ceylon on the morning of the 8th. The whole range of mountains, running inland at a distance of 40 or 50 miles from the coast, including Adam's Peak, was distinctly visible before the sun showed itself above the horizon. On the next day we left Colombo by an afternoon train for Kandy. The rail runs along the flat for nearly three hours, and then commences the ascent of the mountain. With a bogie-engine in front and another behind, the train winds in rapid curves, in a most serpentine fashion, up the incline, occasionally overhanging a perpendicular cliff, and overlooking a vast expanse of country towards the west, till it reaches an altitude of about 1,800 feet, and then it runs level to Kandy. The incline is about 12 miles in length, and the gradient throughout 1 in 45. The ascent, following closely on the admirably-engineered wheel-road, and the scenery and foliage, with the luxuriant parasites and creepers at every turn, is quite one of the remarkable sights of our tour. Apropos of tropical plants, the Botanical Gardens of Peradinia, three miles from Kandy, are a sight worth coming from England to see. They comprise a varied palmery (it is supposed that there are 150 different kinds of palm), fernery and tropical trees and shrubs, the like of which I had never seen before; for instance, splendid groups of the giant bamboo, the mahogany tree, upas tree, Talipot palm with its ragged stem, various kinds of gamboge, cinnamon tree of large growth, magnificent Indian rubber tree, 100 feet high and 20 feet in girth—so different from our slender drawing-room plant—cocoa tree, cardimum, clove,—in short, acres on acres of our choicest hot-house vegetation in the open air. Two of the Talipot palms were in flower; they arrive at maturity in about forty years, flower for the first and only time when at maturity, and then die. I stroll out every night after dinner at Kandy by the margin of the lake and round the green, gazing on the brilliant starlit sky, Orion's belt immediately over head, Sirius and Canopus shining like moons, with a galaxy of bright stars studded thickly in the heavens; below the fire-flies flitting about in the soft warm air, the lights of the bungalows on the hills reflected in the lake, the scene altogether one of surpassing beauty.

This is just now the country for young scapegraces who have made bad starts, or no start at all, in England. Coffee is up, and the whole island is alive with coffee planters, and new ground is being cleared and planted. Everyone in that line is thriving; coffee, which some years ago was 50*s.* the cwt., is now 120*s.*, and coffee estates of 300 or 400 acres are producing a net £10,000 a-year to their proprietors. Kandy is full of young men, who are managers of estates in various parts of the island, the picking season being over they have come down to the town for a spree; these young fellows get their £300 and £400 a-year as managers; they live in small bungalows on the estates, and superintend the labour, which is all done by coolies or natives from Southern India. Often they live in wild upland districts, 20 or 30 miles from a town, and many miles from any European neighbour, and that is the drawback, no society whatever. Consequently, like many of our Welsh hill farmers, when they get down to the town, they go in for a drink and have a regular bout of it. I hear it is so sometimes when they get together at each others' bungalows on special occasions. This island would be an opening for young fellows who could keep straight and abstain from liquoring up. It is a capital opening for a steady industrious young man at the present time. The cinchona is being introduced into the island, quinine is made from its bark, and that and coffee and tea will afford abundant employment for capital and labour for many years to come. There is sport to be had in the island by way of set-off against the solitary life in the districts. Everyone said to me before we set foot in Ceylon, "If you go to Ceylon don't be taken in with precious stones there; don't buy of the hawkers and fellows who come round and offer you coloured glass for rubies and emeralds of the finest water." I was sitting in my bed-room on the ground floor of the Colombo Hotel the second day after our arrival, doors and window wide open, when a Cingalese presented himself in the costume of the country, introduced by the waiter, as villanous an introduction as a man could well have. He said he was a jeweller, and at once proceeded to pull out of his waist-band divers small rolls of cotton cloth, which he untied and unwound, and arranged on the bed heaps of stones, pearls, &c. In the matter of such things I confess to feeling something like a moth round a candle—an absolute and certain conviction that I shall be singed, nay, scorched, burnt up, fried alive, frizzled to death, done for, but yet I cannot resist the attraction. I kept on repeating to the fellow, "No, I don't want them; I don't understand the value; I have spent all my money." He cleverly replied, "Look, sir, you need not buy; I don't want the money; master is a gentleman I see by his face and talk; master take any he likes, take all, and send me the money from London." "Well," at last I said, opening my mouth, like the crow in the fable to the flattery, "what's the price of that pearl ring?" "The lowest price," he replied, "£16." "And that ruby ring?" "£30," he replied. He then produced to me letters from London and Ryder, and from some English gentlemen with whom he had had dealings, which rather re-assured me. "No," I said, "I don't want 'em; but rather than you should go away and have your trouble for nothing, I'll give you £10 for the pearl ring." He refused, and we went on chaffering for half an hour. At last I said, "I will give you £30 for the pearl ring *and* the ruby ring, and if that won't do pack up your things and be off." He took it, and I gave him a cheque for £30, with which he was quite content. The same afternoon I went to Government House to see Sir William Gregory, the Governor, who is collecting precious stones, and knows a good deal about them, and he invited us to see his collection. Who should be closeted with him in his sitting-room but my friend, the Cingalese jeweller! "Halloa!" I said, "that man has been with me to-day, and I have had a deal with him." "You must be careful with all these fellows," Sir William said,—"they'll do you if they can—he's trying now to sell me this cat's-eye (producing a small one not bigger than a pea) for £25—its a fine one, but I must take time to consider. What have you bought?" It so happened that I had the rings on my finger. "Very pretty," he said; "they will be very acceptable at home;" and on being told the price, he added, "you have got well out of his clutches—he hasn't done you so much as I expected."

I miss in Ceylon the demonstrative religion of Southern India. There is very little of the outward and visible sign of religion here—no showy temples, no processions, no beating of tom-toms, no idolatrous or votive images in the villages, no marking of the forehead or of the body with distinctive marks, as with the Hindoos. The Buddhist form of religion struck me as analogous to our Protestant, and the Brahminical to the Romish in our country. The people here are more independent, less servile, and less the victims of priestcraft than in India.

What a lesson to us Christians is the courage of the so-called heathen in their outward observance of religion! It never enters into the head of the Mahommedan or Hindoo to be ashamed of his faith. At all times, and in all places, amidst their daily occupation, in open thoroughfares as well as in mosques and temples, these men may be seen in acts of earnest devotion, abstracting themselves for the time from their immediate business, offering up their sacrifice of prayer or thanksgiving, and then returning to their work as if no human eye had seen them. Not only was this conspicuous with the naked Mahommedan crew in our Paumben boat, who discontinued their work at intervals and united with one accord in prayer as we passed some sacred shrine on the shore, but I have seen it in countless instances throughout the East—natives of both persuasions (not necessarily pilgrims or devotees) prostrating themselves in prayer in the dust along the roads and thoroughfares, sailors kneeling on the decks in ships, Parsees at their orisons under the evening sky, and all whilst the full tide of life and business was surging around them. Among the Hindoos, the larger proportion of men, in Southern India at all events, carry on their foreheads in bright colours the distinctive mark of their religious profession, which mark is carefully put on the forehead every morning after ablution. Surely, setting aside all doctrine, these men must have God's spirit, or some spiritual feeling akin to it, within them!

KANDY, CEYLON,
Sunday, 14th January, 1877.

YOUR long letter, finished on the 14th December, reached me yesterday evening at 9 o'clock. With it came one from dear R., and many other home letters. I read all these with the greatest comfort, and then with a heart open to enjoyment strolled out in the pretty, well-planted green here close by the ornamental water, and watched the fire-flies flitting across my path and lighting up the trees in all directions with innumerable little fires, the balmy night being in keeping with the scene and with my thoughts. By the same post Monier received his Oxford letters, which informed him that he was not expected to return till the middle of March, and that his Institute objects would be better promoted by his absence than if he were to return sooner, distance in fact had had its proverbial effect. We therefore return to Colombo next Tuesday in order to embark in the "Assam" for Bombay direct. We have made out our visit to the Mountain Sanitarium of Newera Ellia. We left this on Thursday morning by rail to Gampola, and then took the wretched rattle-trap called the mail,—35 miles of continual ascent, to Newera Ellia. The road is a series of dangerous zigzags admirably engineered by Skinner, but the journey both up and down in such a conveyance is performed at the risk of one's life, as the edge of the road all through is wholly unprotected against steep declivities. The scenery is very grand, but I was disappointed with Newera Ellia itself. In my letter to Ro I have given him an account of the flourishing state of the coffee districts through which the road passes. The colony is most prosperous, and fortunes are being made by the coffee growers. We returned to Kandy yesterday, having enjoyed one night of sharp cold and a morning of hoar frost at an altitude of 6,400 feet above the sea. As I write now in my bed-room here at 3 p.m., my little thermometer stands at 82°. Such is the difference caused by the locality. But I am delighted with Kandy. It is a perfect little bijou of a town, and so carefully laid out and attended to. The Governor's house (the Pavilion) is simply perfection, with its tropical garden radiant with flowers and brilliant-leaved plants, and the walks about and around on the hills afford abundant pleasure and recreation. I think I could enjoy life at Kandy if I had my belongings with me and my two cobs. I have not seen any place which has "fetched" me more.

The natives here in Ceylon are more Japanese in feature and dress than Indian. They wear an inverted thimble of red and yellow stuff on the head, a short jacket, belt, and cloth round the waist wrapped tight, a semicircular comb on the top of the head to keep the hair back, and always carry a Chinese umbrella. But the coolie immigration almost swamps the native Cingalese. The thoroughfares swarm with coolies going to and from the coffee estates, and with miserable mud-built shops for the supply of their wants. The vegetation here is very beautiful indeed. The island has about 100 inches of rain annually, and more evenly spread over the year than in India.

One meets with strange people occasionally in travelling. On our return journey the other day from Tinnevelly to Tuticorin we changed carriages at the junction, and got into a saloon carriage on the main line whose only occupant was a stout goodlooking man of about fifty. He had light curly hair carefully parted in the middle, and handsome beard and moustache. He was in his shirt-sleeves, reclining on one of the long seats of the carriage, and on the opposite seat was laid out a complete series of dishes containing cold fowl, salad, potatoes, bread, pudding, plantains, with all suitable accompaniments of butter, salt, &c. Directly we appeared he pulled himself together and apologized for monopolizing the carriage. "Come in, pray come in; I've just finished my tiffin. I'll put all these things by into my tiffin-basket in a moment. Try one of these plantains, you'll find them excellent;" and, so saying, he collected his dishes, emptied the bones and débris out of the carriage-window, and packed the utensils in a large wicker tiffin-basket covered with leather, which was evidently his carefully-contrived and constant-travelling companion. Having done that, he put on his clean white jacket with a gilt uniform button, combed his beard, and began to talk to us freely. He had come from Lahore, he said; thence rather rapidly to Madras, stopping here and there. He slept last night at Madura, and was going for the night to the Travellers' bungalow at Tuticorin, intending to cross the next day in the "Arabia" to Ceylon. "No," I said, "you can't go to the Travellers' bungalow at Tuticorin; we have engaged the rooms for ourselves." "That's unlucky," he replied. "Then I must sleep in the verandah." He was so good-humoured about it, that I rejoined, "No, you must not do that; you shall have my room, and I will have a bed put up in the other room with my nephew;" and that was eventually done. "Now, who can you be?" I asked of myself: "but for a slight excess of freedom in manner and talkativeness, I should take you for a general officer on a tour of inspection." This idea was negatived by his telling us that he lived in London, and had been out to India every year for the last five years, landing at Bombay and making the round of all the Presidencies. "Ah, I see," guessed I again to myself, "you must be a traveller for some mercantile house in England; perhaps an agent for the sale of brandy, beer, or light wines or provisions." The elaborate tiffin-basket rather encouraged that conjecture. On arriving at Tuticorin I went off alone to Underwood, the agent for the steamer, to engage our passage to Colombo. Whilst I was so engaged, in walked my stout handsome friend for the same purpose. "Oh," he exclaimed, "Mr. Underwood, is that you? Don't you remember me, Captain Q——, formerly a skipper in the P. & O. service; don't you remember coming home with me in the 'Moultan' from China?" Here was one point solved. Our friend was Captain Q——, formerly a captain in the P. & O. service. We returned together to the wretched Travellers' bungalow, and I made him comfortable in my room there. From thence we adjourned to the little club, where, notwithstanding his substantial repast in the railway carriage, he joined us for tiffin, going through a second meal under that name as if he had tasted nothing all day. We all dined together at the club in the evening, and he had the talk nearly all to himself. Ships, trade, politics, people of all ranks whom he had sailed with, every conceivable subject, interspersed with remarks on the food, quick calls for this or that dish, and a joke now and then with his man-servant Pedro in bad Hindustani.

The next morning early we all walked down together to the beach and embarked in the bullion boat which took us off to the "Arabia." He was one of the only two other passengers we had with us on board that vessel. Nevertheless he was sharp enough to take the best cabin, had the first bath, and secured the best of everything for himself like a practised traveller. In conversation with him on board the "Arabia," I frequently led up to the difficulty which still puzzled me, "You were formerly in the P. & O. service, what are you *now?*" I said to him; "I suppose you were not sorry to leave the service?" "Delighted," he replied, "I had had enough of it. The company cut down our pay. In my time a captain had £1,300 a-year pay, and the best of living on board free. What do you think now? Why, actually every officer has to pay for his liquor—he can't have a bottle of beer without he pays for it. I couldn't stand that. Now I'm my own master and have my own independent occupation." Then he branched off into some other topic, talking all the time with great shrewdness and good humour. We anchored off Colombo early the following morning. I asked Captain Q—— if he was going on shore. "No," he replied, "not yet. I shall have my breakfast comfortably on board; the purser here on this ship gives capital breakfasts; then I shall land and take the afternoon train to Kandy. I've got some business at Kandy." So we left him and remained ourselves in Colombo a couple of days, going on afterwards to Kandy. The very first person we met in the hotel at Kandy was Captain Q——, dressed as usual in a complete suit of pure white with the gilt uniform button all down the jacket, with his diamond ring on his third finger, his radiant face and curly hair and beard looking more captivating than ever. "Oh," he exclaimed, "I am so glad to see you; you'll find this hotel a very good one; the butler is a friend of mine, he will look after you." We had some further conversation; he was going off to some friends 20 miles off, but would return to Kandy; thence he was going to Galle and would in time take the steamer to Madras, and work his way eventually through the north of India back to Bombay. "Well, I thought to myself, you are an indefatigable commission agent, and with your energy and good address I doubt not you sell thousands of pounds of brandy or tinned soups, or whatever else you travel in, and make a good thing of it." He went off in the carriage for his 20 mile journey, and meanwhile we made out our two days' excursion to Newera Ellia. On our return to Kandy yesterday we sat down to 7 o'clock dinner. Captain Q—— had returned also and took the only vacant chair next to me, talking as usual about everything and everybody, with observations thrown in about the dinner. "Why what's this? tinned salmon; here's a bottle of anchovy, but where's the melted butter? Here, Pedro, send the butler to me. My good man (to the butler) always serve melted butter with fish; not now—I can do without it—give me some of that cold butter, but in future remember always melted butter, anchovy cannot be taken alone." Then he went off about his movements, and how he could not come with us because he had business at this place and that. At last my curiosity got the better of me, and I said to him plump, right out, "Pray may I ask, Captain Q——, what business you are now engaged in?" "Oh," he replied smiling, "I'm an ordained minister." "Ordained minister!" I echoed. "Yes, he rejoined, "I really am, but I don't look like one, and (seeing that my surprise had not subsided) I hope you don't think that cheerfulness is inconsistent with such calling." I was quite taken aback, I must say. "But," I inquired, "are you an ordained minister of the Church of England?" "Oh, no," he replied, "I am an ordained minister of the Catholic Apostolic Church in Gordon Square. My mission to India every year is to visit and pray with the scattered members of that congregation; but we are not bigots, we believe in one communion and recognize no denominations. My business, however, is with persons in India in direct connection with the Catholic Apostolic Church, and I am sent from Gordon Square to keep alive in its scattered members the true catholic spirit of Christianity. I have some members here in Kandy—two or three privates of the 57th regiment. I have been praying with them this morning. I have a few at every place I visit, and I seek them out and pray with them individually." And then he expounded his creed (for the first time neglecting his dinner in his zeal) and launched out into the Book of Revelation,—the four Beasts; the Spirit and the Bride; the Second Advent, and a volume of rhapsody. I never was more surprised in my life, as he had not before given the faintest clue to his vocation; and that Gordon Square should have its travelling priest never entered into my head. The character struck me as so novel and interesting that I thought it worth while to give it to you in this detail. He is off now to Colombo, and thence back to Tuticorin, en route for Madras and Calcutta. I have since heard that he is an archangel in the Gordon Square Church.

SS. "Goa," off Goa,
25th January, 1877.

Our plans have undergone a change since I wrote to you from Colombo. We found that the passage money by the "Assam," from Colombo to Bombay, was 120 rupees each; and although I did not myself objeet to that sum, Monier thought it too much to pay for himself and Stanley, seeing that he had a free pass for both by rail. It then became a question what we should do. I had no free pass, and I had already travelled the 1,200 miles of rail from Bombay to Madras and thence to Tuticorin, and a very hot and dusty and uninteresting journey it was. I had no desire to undertake it a second time, so we compromised the matter by giving up the "Assam," and agreeing to take the coasting steamer together to Beypoor, the terminus on the western coast of the Madras Railway, whence we all, or Monier and Stanley at all events, could take the rail to Madras and on to Bombay. The "Goa," belonging to the British India Steam Navigation Company, was anchored off Colombo at the time, and accordingly on Wednesday, the 17th, we put off from Colombo, bag and baggage, and embarked in her. She weighed anchor at 5 o'clock the same evening, arrived at Tuticorin mid-day the next day, rounded the grand headland of Cape Comorin on Friday, anchored off Cochin on Saturday, and off Beypoor on Sunday morning. At this last place Monier and Stanley, with the servant Rama, disembarked early enough in the morning to catch the 10 o'clock train to Salem, on the road to Madras, on the same day. As I have said, I had seen all that line of railway, whereas the Malabar coast and the most interesting places on it I had not seen. The "Goa" was a new and clean ship; I had a good cabin to

Tillecherry Boatman
23 Jany

myself, the table on board was excellent, and the captain a pleasant man; so I resolved to keep by the ship, and here I am still, having been on board eight days, and no part of my tour has been more enjoyable or more varied. I shall miss seeing Hyderabad. Monier said he should endeavour to stop there on his way from Madras to Bombay, but I have been fully compensated by the voyage so far, which has really been a yachting voyage of a delightful kind; the only bit of rough sea was the run across from Colombo to Tuticorin. After passing Tuticorin and rounding Cape Comorin, the western sea is sheltered by the land from the north-eastern monsoon, and it has been a millpond ever since. Besides the sea we had another drawback in the run from Colombo to Tuticorin, in the shape of a cargo of 700 coolies returning to India after the close of the coffee picking season in Ceylon. They were stowed away as thick as herrings between decks, and were all more or less ill during the night; the horrors of the "middle passage," in the old days of negro slavery, over again. It took a deal of cleansing to make the ship sweet again. But it was all over after that night, and since then the ship has been perfect. We have anchored at Colachel, Allipey, Cochin, Beypoor, Calicut, Budagherry, Tillicherry, Cannanore, Mangalore and Carwar, and we are now on our way to the Portuguese Settlement of Goa. Colachel is a collection of mud huts, a large Roman Catholic church, and a smaller Protestant one, with a background of cocoa-nut trees. It is an interesting coast thence to Cochin, with villages and churches and chapels dotted along its whole length, the Syrian Christians having a settlement here, besides the Roman Catholics. At Cochin I landed in the canoe called the mail boat—a pull of about three miles to the entrance to the harbour. It is a narrow and shallow entrance, bounded on all sides by cocoa-nut trees, leading into a considerable extent of backwater, which runs as far as Beypoor to the north, and for 20 or 30 miles to the south. In this backwater numerous bunder boats and native trading craft of very primitive construction were moored, and round it, on the shore, I counted seven or eight large Roman Catholic chapels. But my main object in landing was to visit the colony of white Jews which has been settled here for centuries. A second boat from Cochin jetty took us up the backwater for about two miles to the colony. It is entirely apart from the rest of the town. There are two synagogues, into one of which (being their Sabbath to-day) we were fortunate enough to enter just as service was commencing. Numerous white and unmistakeable Jews were assembled, clothed in silk of the most brilliant colours—crimson, emerald green, purple, striped, &c. In the centre of the square room which formed the synagogue, and which was hung with chandeliers and oil lamps, there was a roomy, open pulpit, into which after a time one rabbi, and then three together, entered, veiled themselves, and stood. Then was brought out to them with ceremony, from a closet over what we should call the altar, a circular case containing a double roll of parchment, the Book of the Law, from which one of the rabbis read, intoning, the congregation, also veiled, responding. This was followed by silent prayer, the congregation standing in rows and all facing the altar. The parchment rolls were afterwards restored to the case; the congregation gathering round the case to kiss or touch it before it was put back into the closet. The chief rabbi told me that there were 200 white Jews in Cochin, and about 1,000 black Jews, but he could give me no reliable information as to the origin of the colony. A large proportion of the native population of Cochin is Roman Catholic. The Protestant proportion includes chiefly the British residents, who assemble in a large, rude and imposing-looking old building, with massive buttresses, interesting as containing the tomb of Vasco di Gama. The fort of Cochin belongs to the British, but the district is under an independent rajah. It is the seat of a brisk trade, chiefly in cocoa-nuts, the fibre and oil, and coffee, grown in the Travancore mountains. I landed also at Tillicherry, Cannanore, Mangalore and Carwar, and walked about each of these places for three or four hours. Each place has a character of its own; the natives vary, at each place, their costume, boats, &c., so that the interest of the voyage is kept up the whole time; and the magnificent outline of the western Ghauts, which stretch the whole way from Cape Comorin to Bombay, is in view from first to last, the shadows and colours on the mountains affording a constant treat to the eye in the way of landscape. After landing and roaming about, I return to the clean ship, roomy cabin and good food (the meals all being served on deck) with great satisfaction. From Beypoor to Mangalore we had Mr. Powell, a local barrister, and Mrs. Palmer, the wife of the bank manager there, on board. They invited me to land with them at Mangalore, and to breakfast at Mrs. Palmer's bungalow. This I did, and Mr. Powell afterwards drove me in his trap round the town. I had before landed with him at Tillicherry, a very original native place, which, so far as the streets and people are concerned, looked as if no European had ever landed there, were it not for the remains of certain old Portuguese forts, which conjure up the ghosts of Vasco di Gama or some of his enterprising contemporaries. Before touching at Cannanore, we passed the small French Settlement of Mahé, which appears to consist of nothing but the governor's house and a flag-staff. I have always some excitement in landing. Except at Carwar, there is no natural harbour on the western coast between Galle and Bombay; consequently, the ship anchors always in the open roadstead, about three miles from the shore; the native boats which come out for passengers are of the rudest kind, often only a canoe scooped out of the trunk of a tree; sometimes a catamaran, with a log of wood rigged out by a couple of bamboo poles to keep the thing from capsizing; sometimes a flat-bottomed canoe, with the planks only sewn together, the crew, oars and tackle being all in keeping and most original. At first, I was somewhat uneasy at trusting myself in such rotten concerns, but I am now used to it, and admire the skill of the naked savages who navigate them, and who chatter and sing the whole time with great vehemence. In returning from Mangalore to the ship yesterday, when I was quite alone, I really thought we should never get back to the ship, as a strong head-wind had sprung up, and our canoe tumbled about over the bar which we had to cross, the sea breaking over us; but the black fellows pulled away with their bamboo oars, singing and encouraging each other, and I got on board at last. We have to touch at Goa, Vingorla and Rutnagherry, before arriving at Bombay.

Friday, 26th Jan. We did not anchor in the Goa river last night. The town of Goa is six miles up the river; too far off, even if we had anchored. I was sorry not to see it, as I am told it is a quaint old place. The Portuguese officer in charge of the old fort at the entrance to the river came off to us in full uniform, and when he had taken off his cap on deck and backed down the ladder to his boat again, we steamed off to Vingorla, and anchored there at 8 p.m. Here we took on board the young Rajah of Sawunt Warree, with his suite, and a tag-rag and bob-tail of natives besides. It was a pretty sight to see these boats coming off to the ship in the night, with torches, which lit up the bright turbans and dresses of the young rajah and his followers. The embarkation of passengers and cargo, and cluster of native boats round the ship, and chatter of the naked crew, with the sparkling lights and reflections on the sea, is always an amusing sight, especially at night. The rajah, a boy of about fourteen, occupies himself by reclining at full length on the top of the skylight on deck, propped up with cushions, and playing at chess with his retainers. He is on his way to the college at Rajcote, the principal of which is Mr. Macnaghten, who came out with us in the "Nepaul;" and a very happy thing it is for these effeminate young native princes that there is such a training place for them. We were off again in the night, and are now anchored off Rutnagherry, a pretty little bay, protected by a bold headland, to the north. I sat for a couple of hours on the bridge of the ship last night, after we left Vingorla, enjoying the tropical night; my only companion was the officer of the watch. The moonlight gave a mysterious prominence to the dangerous reef called the Vingorla Rocks, which runs out at right angles from the shore for about ten miles. Not long since, the "Candia," a fine vessel belonging to this company, was wrecked on the reef. They have just lost another vessel, the "Dacca," on a sunken reef off the Coromandel coast. Rutnagherry is our last anchorage, the next is Bombay Harbour.

Bombay, Saturday, 27th. Entered Bombay Harbour and anchored at 8 o'clock this morning, and sorry I was to bring my yachting voyage to a close—it has been a very pleasant interlude in my tour. Just as we anchored, I descried L. Fletcher in a shore-boat coming off for me. I collected my effects, and put them and myself into his boat, and we landed very comfortably. He kindly insisted on my taking up my quarters at his house on Malabar Hill.

After all the experience I have had of India I have seen no place so attractive, geographically, as Bombay, unless it be Kandy. I stood on the bridge of the "Goa" from 5.30 this morning, long before sunrise, until she anchored at 8, and was enchanted with the lovely harbour and all the adjuncts of English shipping and native craft, islands, cocoa-nut trees, ghauts, &c. But with all this, again I say, old England for me. I cannot live without exercise, and no exercise is really enjoyable in this climate, which is made only for rajahs and such like, who recline on ottomans and are waited upon by slaves.

MALABAR HILL, BOMBAY,
Friday, 2nd February, 1877.

THIS, I suppose, will be my last letter to you, at all events, from India. It will go by the mail of the 5th. We, I hope, follow ourselves by the next mail, that of the 12th. After I had posted my last letter to you, in which I left the actual day of our departure somewhat uncertain, I received Monier's expected letter, written from Madras, in which he said that if I would wait for the P. & O. Co.'s steamer "Surat," leaving Bombay on the 12th, he and Stanley would accompany me. I always told him that I would go by the "Surat" if he resolved on that steamer also, and therefore, on the receipt of his letter, I went to the P. & O. office and secured berths for the "Surat;" but there was no occasion for booking beforehand, as she will not probably carry more than fifty passengers this voyage, and she makes up 200 berths. I hope we may each of us have a cabin to himself, as a separate cabin makes all the difference in the comfort of the voyage. The "Surat" goes through the Canal to Southampton, but we shall leave her at Suez, and take the route home by Brindisi. I do not think we shall stay at Cairo, but this I cannot determine until I see Monier. I heard from him a second time yesterday from Hyderabad. He and Stanley were quartered at the Residency, and were overwhelmed with state and grandeur; but the railway journey there must have been troublesome, as they had to sleep at station-houses more than once owing to delay in the trains. They expect to be in Bombay on Sunday night; and we all start together for Ellora and Ajunta on Tuesday night, returning to Bombay on the following Saturday in time to pack up and settle for our embarkation in the "Surat" on the 12th. In the meantime, I am enjoying myself here, with all the comforts of home, as the guest of Lancie and his wife. The bungalow, though small, is extremely pretty, commanding a beautiful peep of the sea, from which there is generally a fresh breeze. The ordinary life of persons here is to get up at daylight, 6.30; the first toilet is a rough one, because what exercise is taken, such as a ride on horseback, lawn tennis, &c., comes off then. But before going out there is tea and toast ready as soon as you leave your bedroom at 7. Then there is an interval of two hours or two hours and a half for exercise, or letter-writing, or any other occupation, at the expiration of which comes the bath and grand toilet, followed by a substantial breakfast in regular courses. In my case I have, after breakfast, always accompanied Lancie into the town in his dog-cart, either to transact business or see sights, and have either driven the dog-cart back myself or come back in a hack buggy to tiffin with Gertrude at 2. It is four miles from this house to the heart of the town. Then the custom is for the wives of the business men, who are in fact all the men of the community, to leave their homes at 5 o'clock in the evening in their smart carriages, fetch their husbands at their respective offices or places of business, and adjourn to the Apollo Bunder or to the rink for the general rendezvous and gossip, driving home in the dark in time for an 8 o'clock dinner. The carriages of an evening and the dresses of the ladies are of the smartest, and I should fancy there was a good deal of money spent in that way when it cannot be conveniently afforded. Everybody here amongst the English is very much on a level; the community is composed of persons coming from the same class and mixing in the same social circle in England, that is to say, merchants, brokers, barristers, solicitors, government officials, civilians, working military men, all bees of the same hive, having a common object to make money. There is no aristocracy, and consequently no class distinctions as in our provincial life in England. But I think the spirit of rivalry is rather fostered by the equality, because what Mrs. A. has in the way of equipage or dress, Mrs. B., who is, or believes herself to be, the equal of A., must have also. Certainly all the gentry in Bombay have charming bungalows in the best suburbs, the smartest of barouches and liveries, and lead the gayest of lives. I except Lancie and Gertrude, who keep only a brougham and dog-cart, and do not entertain. I have no doubt the climate suits Lancie and Gertrude equally well. To some constitutions it must be far better adapted than the changes and damp of England. But, again, I say it is not sufficiently brisk and invigorating for me, and, with all her faults, I prefer the old country. Lancie's establishment here consists of a Portuguese male cook; a butler, whose wages are 20 rupees a month, he finding himself in food, clothing, &c.; a boy in the house (under the butler), who goes by the name of chokra, or youngster; an ayah, who is Gertrude's lady's maid, 17 rupees a month, she finding herself in food, clothing, &c.; the hammal, or odd man, who dusts the rooms, sweeps out the verandah, polishes up about a dozen brass idols which Lancie has in various parts of the drawing-room —on certain feast days these idols are found placed in a row with flowers stuck into them and rice placed before them, the old hammal doing all the honour to them he can; two men in the stable, one for each horse; and, lastly, the molli or gardener. It must be such a comfort to have nothing to do with the food or lodging of servants. When Lancie leaves India, as he proposes to do in March for nine or ten months, all the servants are discharged; but he says the very day he returns they will all be found on the wharf where he lands asking to be taken back into service again.

Quite an Indian institution is the borah, or pedlar; shops are not common in India—indeed they don't exist at all except at the capitals; the borah is the peripatetic shop. He comes round to the various houses, on foot generally, on a Sunday, when he knows the sahib to be at home, accompanied or rather followed by three or four coolies, each carrying an enormous pack on his head. He speaks English and approaches the open verandah, where the family may be seated, with "Master want any Cashmere goods, Rampoor Chudder shawls, silks? I got all new goods; master look, master need not buy." The coolies deposit their loads and seat themselves on their haunches at the further end of the portico. Then pack No. 1 is untied by the clever borah, and the contents by degrees strew the floor of the verandah in rich profusion. If a bargain is attempted to be made, a price offered less than the price asked, the borah, with the air and gravity of a lord chancellor, replies, "I make one price; master not like me to have two prices—one price; I make 5 per cent. on my goods, not more; I have one price;" and so on. Then, in most admired confusion, pack No. 2 is untied, and the most gorgeous table and chair covers are exhibited; some worked in gold and silver from Hyderabad in Scinde, dressing gowns, slippers. All these are piled up on the shawls and silks and brocades of pack No. 1, until the verandah is literally heaped up with beautiful things. Who can resist such temptation or the calm face and dignified assurance of the accomplished borah? I know of no pleasure so perfect and enjoyed with such absolute ease and tranquillity as reclining in an armchair, with ladies about you in other armchairs, in a large spacious verandah with a temperature of about 80°, looking languidly at the beautiful Eastern things which the borah brings out one by one from his pack and holds up for your approval, the ladies passing their comments on such articles as are peculiarly within their province. The purchases over, but not till several hours have been thus whiled away, the borah folds up his goods, commenting on them all the time; they are replaced in the packs, and the packs are tied up, and he and his coolies walk away from the precincts as they came. But the borah I speak of belongs to a superior class. He is dressed in pure flowing white, with a compact white turban on his head, his forehead neatly marked in red or yellow with the distinctive mark of his creed, and handsome turquoise or other rings on his fingers. His manner is perfect; squatted on the floor of the verandah he loses none of his dignity, and succeeds in impressing you with a belief (not always well founded) that he is honest and trustworthy. Of course, there are others that are unmitigated rogues.

Driving home to Malabar Hill one night, we were lucky enough to meet in the native town the marriage procession of a couple of young Bunniahs, got up on no ordinary scale. It consisted of a long line of open carriages filled with the friends and family of the two young bridegrooms, the young children in the carriages being dressed out in brilliant gold and silver-spangled dresses and caps, carts with musicians, brass bands, drums and tomtoms on foot, making noise enough to awaken the dead, led horses, caparisoned à la circus, carrying very young children got up in keeping; indeed, it seemed a matter of necessity that every member of both families, both old and young, should follow, for behind these led horses came a crimson velvet and gilt palanquin containing an infant apparently only just born; then paced a couple of extra caparisoned horses carrying the two bridegrooms, effulgent with gold and silver lace and spangles, red umbrellas being held over their heads. These were followed by about fifty adult friends on foot, headed by Sir Mungoldass Nathobhoy, and all dressed in white; then the private carriages of the friends and more music and tomtoms, the whole line being flanked by torch-bearers, or, more correctly, by men and boys carrying iron rods with cradles at the top in which were heaps of pitch or other inflammable materials, sending forth volumes of smoke and flame on all sides. The streets were densely crowded with spectators, and the balconies and windows of the houses also. The bridegrooms were going forth to meet their respective brides. It is said that fortunes are spent in these marriage displays, and here we had proof of the fact, not in the procession alone, but in the brilliantly decorated and illuminated pavilions, erected expressly for the occasion, where the bridegrooms and friends assemble in the first instance preparatory to the start, and to which they afterwards return—a costly ceremony from beginning to end, and certainly, so far as the discordant music is concerned, one more honoured in the breach than in the observance.

SS. "Surat," Gulf of Aden,
19th February, 1877.

A good bit on my way home now, and I am delighted to find myself hourly progressing homewards. I wrote to you by the mail leaving Bombay on the 5th. The next vessel, the "Surat," conveys this letter as well as ourselves to Suez. She left Bombay on the evening of Monday, the 12th. We have had a prosperous run across the Indian Ocean of six days and four hours, and cast anchor in Aden Bay last night at 11.30. Immediately afterwards the P. & O. agent came on board and brought me your two letters. At Suez a grand divergence ensues. We leave the "Surat" there, and take the rail to Cairo; the mail and many of the passengers proceed direct to Alexandria and thence to Brindisi, and the ship itself goes through the Canal to Southampton. Our tour in India was well wound up with Ellora—it is an out-of-the-way place—a night on the rail from Bombay to Nandgaum, and thence forty-five or fifty miles of road to Roza, the Mahommedan town situated on the summit of the high range of hills in the face of which are the celebrated caves. Sir Salar Jung had directed that Monier should be assisted in his visit to the caves, which lie in the dominions of the Nizam, and that a tonga with relays of ponies should be ready to convey us from the station at Nandgaum to Roza. But, unluckily, the tongas had been previously engaged by some officers of the Contingent at Aurungabad, and we were doomed to perform the road journey from Nandgaum to Roza in my old enemies, the bullock bandies. For fifteen hours we were incarcerated in these wretched vehicles, and, to add to the misery as well as the mockery, we had for the whole distance an escort of a couple of mounted Sowars, who walked their horses at a foot's pace by the side of the bullocks. I swore by all the Hindoo gods that no temples or caves, that no sight on the face of the earth or inside of it, would ever induce me to enter a bullock bandy again; but really when I saw Ellora and the marvels of art which were there exhibited to my view I recanted, and was glad that I had committed myself only to Vishnu or Siva, for neither of whom do I care a brass farthing. At Roza we were met by Mr. Burgess, the antiquary, who is engaged in writing an account of the Ellora Caves, and by the agents of Sir Salar Jung, who had prepared the bungalow for our reception. The town of Roza is situated on the plateau of the range of hills in the face of which are the Caves of Ellora. The town is essentially Mahommedan, and has been built of solid rectangular stones brought from the ancient city of Tagara, but is itself now falling into ruins. Within the cupola'd walls is the tomb of Aurungzebe, plain and open to the sky, but entered through doors of perforated marble. The other tombs, within and without the walls, are of different holy men and of kings of Hyderabad, all constructed with a central dome, flanked by minarets, and very beautiful in form and execution. Many of the stone slabs at the entrance to these tombs were inlaid with lumps of agate, glass and coloured stones, as votive offerings from various individuals; and against the doors were nailed horse-shoes, with a like object. We, in England, have the same custom with regard to horse-shoes; and Mr. Burgess thinks it was introduced from the East into England by the Crusaders. In the East it is an offering by a soldier who has been promoted to a rank which entitles him to keep a horse. Descending from the town of Roza to the face of the hill, we came upon the Ellora Caves. There is one temple at Ellora, which is not a cave or a cavern, but a vast independent structure standing

P. 145.

p 145.

out in the open as if built, stone on stone, according to the most approved principles of architecture; and yet this temple, with its obelisks, colossal elephants and subsidiary temples outside, and its halls, vestibules, galleries, storeys, staircases, inside, is hewn entirely out of the solid rock, from which it is wholly separate and apart, as much so as St. Paul's is from the houses which surround it; and the detail of carving which covers every part of the outside and inside is as much part of the marvel as the edifice itself. This temple is called Kailasa, and is only one of sixty-five wonderful works which comprise the caves or temples of Ellora. They are cut in the face of the range of trap hills which rise abruptly out of the plain in a semicircular form, the earliest in date, about A.D. 300, being Buddhist, and cut in the southern horn of the semicircular range; the next or intermediate, both in place and date, being Brahminical or Hindoo, and the most modern, Jain, about A.D. 900; the last being cut in the northern horn of the range. The trap formation of the hills, consisting of large, horizontal slabs of rocks, is favourable to excavation, the slabs forming naturally the floor and roof of the temple. Many of the temples run for nearly 200 feet into the solid rock, and consist of two and three floors, supported by pillars of the most exquisite design and execution, and all round the walls are bas-reliefs, illustrating the gods of the Hindoo mythology in almost every phase of their history. The date of Kailasa is about A.D. 700. More of this when we meet. I could fill volumes if I once commenced on a description. Ajunta, we were told, was equally remarkable, but it was 90 miles off by road; and oh! those bullock bandies!—it would have been *a-jolt-a* as well as Ajunta; besides, we had not the time; so instead, as tongas had now been provided for us by the Nizam's agents for the particular journey, we proceeded to the extraordinary fortress of Dowlutabad, thence on to Aurungabad, formerly the Nizam's capital, and so back to Nandgaum. Of all impregnable places, at all events before the invention of the 100-ton gun, Dowlutabad must surely rank the first. Picture to yourself a tall wedding cake placed on a flat dining-room table, and an army of pigmies an inch high marching to capture the sugar ornament at the top of the cake. That ornament is the fortress at the top of a rock rising perpendicularly on all sides out of the plain, an inland Gibraltar in fact, and entered only by zigzag galleries capable of admitting only two or three abreast, cut out of the solid rock, with precautions for roasting and boiling the head of the assaulting column, at certain intervals in those galleries, such as would only enter into the head of a native. I could never have imagined such natural and artificial defences. At Aurungabad, as I have been unable to visit the Taj at Agra, I was glad to see the marble tomb to the wife of Aurungzebe, said to be an imitation of the Taj. These interesting sights being done, we made a night journey in a tonga with relays of ponies, and escorted by relays of sowars, to join the rail at Nandgaum, and thence back to Bombay. I returned to my quarters on Malabar Hill with Lancie. Then, on the afternoon of the 12th, I met Monier at the Apollo Bunder; and, accompanied by Lancie and his wife and by Evan James, we all crossed the harbour to the "Surat," our friends kindly coming to see us off. I have left Bombay with the impression that, take it for all in all, it is the pleasantest place to live in that I have visited in India, excepting of course the Sanitariums; but I was not sorry, charmed and excited as I have been with my whole tour, to see the beautiful flashing light of "the Prongs" off Colaba Point gradually fade in the distance as the "Surat" steamed away into the darkness of the Indian Sea. This vessel is, though old, roomy and comfortable; and, as there are only fifty or sixty passengers on board, each passenger has a cabin to himself, and that is an enormous privilege. I have, however, been compelled to change my cabin, an ancient rat having appropriated my first quarters, and having taken into his head to visit my feet and toes every night by way of remonstrance against my intrusion. I could not get rid of him, and very unpleasant it was to feel him running over me in the dark, for I had no covering but a sheet, and so I beat a retreat, and hope to be free for the future. A good table is kept on board. The captain (Burne), a pleasant, gentlemanlike man, an Irvingite, like our friend the Archangel; but this did not prevent him from giving us two services according to our Prayer Book, on deck yesterday, morning and evening, he himself officiating, and reading and singing uncommonly well. We have become friends, and I was with him on the bridge of the ship all last night (always a great delight to me), as she felt her way under the shadow of the huge jagged cinder rock of Aden, and took up her anchorage at 11.30 in the bay. There is something grand and mysterious in the approach to a frowning rock like this from the sea in the middle of a dark night, no sound audible but the wash of the sea against the bows of the ship and the sharp word of command to the men at the wheel. Now we are steaming for the Straits of Bab-el-Mandib, and I will reserve the rest of my letter till we are nearer Suez.

Red Sea, 20th Feb. We are fairly on our way to Suez, being now about 300 miles from Aden and 900 from Suez; very warm it is—85° in the companion and 90° in my cabin, which is on the port or wrong side of the ship; but I cannot complain—the voyage has been delightful thus far, and with pleasant companions. My friends in England cannot say that I have neglected them in the way of correspondence, and often under difficulties, as at present, seated as I now am in my cabin with the blotting-book on my knee, the whole ship trembling from stem to stern with the vibrations of the screw, my hand exuding at every finger, and clinging to the paper under a temperature of 90°; and all this in addition to my Journal, which I have kept strictly from day to day. Tell Pickett that I have eaten Indian curries every day since I left England—some made by the best native cooks in Bombay and Madras, and not one can come up to her dry curry—hers is better to my taste than any of them. The fact is, that in India it is not possible to get either good or tender meat; the meat, never good or fat, is cooked on the day it is killed, never has time to get cold, and comes to table like the sole of an old boot. At the same time, it is quite surprising what native cooks can do with their rude utensils and appliances. Give them three stones and a couple of earthenware pots, and they want nothing else; and here, in this ship, we have the most elaborate meals, with pastry, confectionery, cakes, buns, ices, all thrown in, out of a galley on deck measuring about 8 feet by 6 feet. I forget whether I told you in a former letter that I have tasted the mango both on board the "Goa" when off the Malabar coast and in Bombay. It has a flavour so peculiarly its own, and so agreeable to me, that I for one should give it the palm over all fruits if I had a really fine one and in season. All other Indian fruits are, to my mind, infinitely inferior to ours in England. We have had a prosperous voyage, with no sea except for a few hours off the Gulf of Cambay on starting and to-day as we are entering the Gulf of Suez with a northerly wind against us. I feel now very much like coming home, and the temperature freshens and becomes more English every mile we approach the North.

Cairo, Friday Night,
2nd March, 1877.

How clever you have been in hitting off our movements, and that in the face of much uncertainty, attributable to our frequent change of plans. On our arrival here last Sunday evening I was gladdened, and, I must say, surprised, at finding letters awaiting me at Shepheard's Hotel. I did not expect them, and was therefore the more pleased. I think now that I have received *every* letter which has been written to me from England, and that is some consolation to the writer, and much more to the receiver. No one in England can realize the pleasure of receiving home letters by the absentee in foreign lands, or the grief at having missed his home letters. You will to-day or to-morrow receive the two letters which I wrote and posted to you, the one on board the "Surat" just before we anchored off Suez, and the other at Suez the day following, acknowledging the receipt of your Suez budget. The next day (Sunday) we took the train from Suez to Cairo, a slow but not tedious journey of ten hours. We were in the same carriage with Mr. Le Mesurier, who was also our fellow passenger on board the "Surat," and who is one of the three commissioners appointed by the Khedive to reorganize his railways and ports. Not before it is wanted; for, even after our experience of a day, it was apparent that his highness's railway system was at its lowest ebb. No punctuality; the carriages of the worst construction, dirty inside, and the outside cracking and splintering for want of paint; the whole world admitted to the platforms of all the stations, and every one exacting his utmost from the harassed traveller; whilst blind, ophthalmic, and deformed beggars blocked up the doors and windows of the carriage;

the only remedy being for the traveller to bolt out and lay about him on all sides with a stick. "By heaven!" I said to Le Mesurier, "you have got your work cut out for you for some time to come." For us casuals, however, it was all novelty and amusement. Water carriers, veiled orange women, vendors of sugar cane, Bedouin Arabs, whole families squatted on the floor with their goods and chattels, the women closely veiled, waiting for a train; camels, instead of hack cabs, as at Euston, delivering their burthens or waiting for those expected by the train. These were the incidents of every station we stopped at from Suez to Cairo. And then, about an hour before we reached our destination, the great Pyramids of Ghizeh appeared in sight, followed by the mosques and minarets of Cairo. But the chief characteristics of the journey were the desert, and the rapid and sharply defined transition from the burning sand to the rich, luxuriant fertility of the delta of the Nile. Half way was desert, with nothing but sand; the other half, green corn, thick crops of luzern and clover, beans in full bloom, and the most luxuriant crops of all kinds, with the operations of agriculture in full swing. Just to the line where the Nile overflows was abundant fertility, all beyond that a howling wilderness. We have now had nearly a week in Cairo. I must say it is the most amusing city I have seen in my wanderings. It is a thing by itself, and cannot be compared with the cities of India. The streets and bazaars are entirely different, and every figure one meets differs from the other as much as the Egyptian population differs from the Indian. An attempt has been made by the Khedive to spoil the town by new boulevards in the style of those in Paris. These are not worthy of a visit. The old town, however, is most curious; some of the streets and bazaars so narrow that three persons abreast block up the thoroughfare; but here, nevertheless, you meet camels with their burthens, donkeys with every class of rider, from the turbaned swell with his radiant costume to the lowest peasant in brown sackcloth; women, sometimes on foot, sometimes riding astride on donkeys, in black balloon-like silk coverings, always veiled; itinerant traders, changers of money, fortune-tellers—I cannot say what besides. Many of these streets are covered over with planks, from the top of one house to the top of the other opposite, for shade. These loose planks admit of a fitful light, which catches the brilliant colours of the dresses below or the wares or fruits in the shops, and presents a subject for the artist, unequalled, I should say, anywhere else. Donkeys are the great institution in Cairo. They stand for hire at the corner of every street in hundreds, most of them gaily caparisoned. Everyone rides. It is the only mode in which you can thread your way along the narrow crowded thoroughfares. The intelligent little animal ambles along, the easiest and safest of paces, about five miles an hour, whilst the donkey-boy behind cries out to all in front to make room, or now and then takes the donkey by the head to steer you through a difficulty. The donkey-boy is himself an animal by himself. He speaks a little English, and is proud to show you the lions and the special capabilities of his donkey. He does not spare himself, and will run the whole day behind the donkey, and the faster you all go the better he is pleased. Our two boys have found out the relationship we three stand to each other. Yesterday, my fellow was chattering in Arabic to some friend, and I, in my curiosity, asked him, "Hassan, what are you saying?" He replied, "Notin (nothing), oh, my uncle." They were resolved that the animals should exhibit their paces. Yesterday, during a sharp canter along a dusty road, I heard a bump and a thump, and looked round and saw Stanley rolling on the ground in a cloud of dust—the pace had been too good for him, and he rolled off in the canter, but fortunately fell on his ample pays bas, and sustained no damage except a shock to his dignity. We have been to the Pyramids of Ghizeh. The road crosses the Nile over a new iron bridge at Boulac, and then runs through avenues of acacia, and past two of the many large new palaces recently built for the Khedive's sons (thus have the new Egyptian loans been squandered !), for about 8 miles, to the Pyramids. These consist of the Great Pyramid of Cheops, the Pyramid Belzoni close to it, and two or three smaller ones. They are all placed on a plateau of sand above the level of the valley. The smooth casing stones have been removed from all, and the outline is consequently broken into the rugged squares composing the next course of masonry. The size of these squares can only be appreciated when one is close to them, and the size of one square of stone then conveys a just idea of the gigantic proportion of the whole Pyramid. We were, of course, pestered by the Arabs of the adjacent village, who claim the Pyramids as their perquisite, first to induce us to ascend the large Pyramid, and then to penetrate into the interior. With difficulty, and sometimes on all fours, I contrived to crawl inside as far as the first chamber, and here with the aid of a candle I verified the fact of the squares of stone inside being so exactly fitted that the join was scarcely discernible. You know the theory advanced by Mr. John Taylor and by Professor Piazzi Smyth, that the Great Pyramid was built by the Shepherd Kings 4,000 years and more ago, not as a place of sepulture, but as the repository for certain standard measures and distances; its height, base, cubic contents, passages, chambers, &c. symbolizing and perpetuating important figures in mensuration, as, for instance, the orbit of the earth round the sun, the precession of the equinoxes, the distance of the sun from the earth. How do they account, then, for the fact of there being several pyramids and all of different sizes? But I am not armed for learned controversy, and decline to enter into the lists on either side.

On my exit from the Great Pyramid I gave my two attendants a rupee each in addition to the two rupees exacted from each traveller by the sheik of the village according to tariff. One of my attendants happened to be an outsider, and the rupee I gave him was the cause of intense jealousy to the orthodox village Arabs, who set upon him, his own father, the most violent of the aggressors, falling on and biting him in the face. A general skrimmage ensued, in which I joined, and belaboured the old father with my cane to rescue his son from his clutches. The vast mounds of rubbish, broken pottery, stone and bricks which surround the Pyramids and cover the sphinx and subterranean temples are evidence of the existence of a large town and population at this spot in former days. A longer excursion still we afterwards took to the Pyramids of Sakarah, and we have examined the interesting museum here and visited the mosques, Coptic churches, &c., but I do not intend to afflict you with a page out of Murray. To-day we spent two hours with the Howling Dervishes, certainly a most extraordinary spectacle. In a large mosque with a domed roof were collected about forty of these men, seated in the form of a horseshoe, the centre figure at the base being the chief priest. First they recited or intoned certain sentences all together, and all swaying their bodies to and fro in unison, being all seated on their hams. By degrees they changed the words and took up another chant in a more excited strain, with now and then a sharp whoop or yell—then they all took off their turbans and outer robes, and all stood up arrayed in various coloured gowns, their long hair flowing down behind their backs. Now commenced an extraordinary scene of excitement. One of the number placed himself in the centre of the horseshoe, and gave vent to a deep gasp from the very pit of the stomach, repeating the gasp as often as he could regain his breath. All the rest gasped or groaned in chorus after him, at the same time bending their bodies forward to the ground and then suddenly backwards, their long hair falling first forward over their faces, and then, by the sudden movement of the body backwards, being tossed violently behind their backs. No words were used, but these deep gasps or groans of the most unearthly tone, the leader first and then all the rest following in chorus, with the violent movement backwards and forwards of the body. So excited did they at last become that two of the number dropped senseless on the floor. I should say that towards the end, to heighten the frantic noise, there was a drum accompaniment, and the leader in the centre was changed to make room for other and fresher men, who gave the gasp in another key, followed by the chorus with renewed vigour. During a part of the time one of the number, dressed in white, whirled round and round for a full quarter of an hour, after the manner of the dancing dervishes, he being one of that persuasion. No money was taken at the door, and none was asked for or expected. The men seemed earnest and devout in their worship, and I can only suppose that an ecstatic communion with the Deity was the object they had in view in such worship. This extraordinary scene lasted for two hours. I wished I had talent enough to paint the scene—it was so unique and so striking and dramatic. In the evening I walked to the Citadel to have a last panoramic view, under a setting sun, of the city, the Nile and the Pyramids from the terrace. On my way through the crowd, at the foot of the mosque of Sultan Hassan, I saw a gawky Egyptian soldier, with his mouth wide open, drinking in words which were being whispered into his ear by a sharp, clever-looking man, with books and writing materials next to him, the two being seated side by side. We had a Coptic boy with us who spoke English, and I asked the boy what those two men were doing. "That soldier," the boy replied, "is having his fortune told." We walked up to the men, and then I learnt, through my little Coptic interpreter, that the fortune-teller, a regular profession by the way, had been promising the soldier thirteen houris in Paradise. The poor wretch had some claim to a happy future, as his pay on earth was at the most a piastre, or twopence, a day. However, I was seized with the desire to know something of my own destiny under such encouragement, and begged the fortune-teller to turn his attention to me. He deliberately opened an Arabic book, the pages of which were divided into small squares, and desired me to place my finger on one of the squares. I did so. He then looked at the palm of my hand, and with great apparent study consulted some of his other books, took a slip of paper, and having jotted down my fortune on it in Arabic characters, handed it to me gravely as his decision past all appeal or revocation. The interpretation was as follows: "He seeks for a difficult thing, and he shall have it. The sorcerer will pray to the evil spirits that they may obtain it for him, and that is one houri for a wife." Here was a great falling off, and I showed my disappointment, much to the amusement of a large crowd who had gathered round us, and who were evidently keenly interested in my fate. But I think I made some advance in public favour, and certainly added to the merriment, by asking the soldier if he could not adjust the balance, and spare me two of his houris hereafter. He, taking it all in earnest, replied that I might have two of his with pleasure, and he would keep the remaining eleven; and so the assemblage dispersed, mutually contented, edified and amused. The scene would have furnished a chapter in the "Arabian Nights' Entertainments."

Alexandria, Sunday, 4th March. We arrived here last night, and are now waiting for the Brindisi passengers from Suez to embark on board the "Avoca," which is waiting for us in the harbour. But the weather has changed for the worse. A westerly gale set in at Cairo yesterday morning, blowing the sand in from the desert to an extent which made it impossible to walk out, and the whole horizon towards the west was of a deep yellow colour from the sand taken up by the wind. All along the line of railway yesterday the sand was most annoying, the gale blowing with a force which rocked the carriages. Partly from the wind, partly from an influx of Australian passengers at Benha Junction, and partly from the national indifference to time, our train was more than three hours late, and instead of arriving here at 7.45, we did not arrive till 11 o'clock. Very cold and very dirty we were. We have had a walk in the town this morning, which is more French than Egyptian, with squares and wide streets, and glass-fronted shops, bearing no resemblance to Cairo; and we have been to church, and have seen also Cleopatra's Needle, and the sister obelisk lying in a horizontal position close by the Cleopatra, and which is about to be transported to the Thames Embankment—not worth the expense I should say, as the sharpness of the sculpture has been defaced, and the whole affair looks worn and damaged. But we are unsettled, not knowing whether we are to embark to-morrow morning or not. At present the Suez mail has not been telegraphed.

Monday, 5th March. We were in despair, there being no telegram from Suez this morning, and the P. & O. agent here could give us no consolation. He certainly feared that the Suez steamer had broken down, in which case our stay here would have been indefinite. However, to our great relief, the much-expected telegram arrived at noon to-day, and we have orders to embark on board the "Avoca" this evening, and she sails for Brindisi early to-morrow (Tuesday) morning. The delay has been really very beneficial, as the gale has, in the meantime, subsided, and we may expect a reasonably fair passage.

SS. "Avoca,"
Friday,
9th March.

We have had a tempestuous voyage—three days and three nights of abject misery. We steamed out of Alexandria Harbour at 8 a.m., Tuesday morning, hoping that the gale was over, and so it was for a few hours. That night it commenced to blow again from the north-west, and we have had a gale in our teeth ever since, with heavy squalls of hail, a tempestuous sea, as bad as we had it in the Bay of Biscay, and for a longer time. Three-fourths of the passengers in bed. All the ports closed, and "fiddles" or guards at table at every meal. This is just one of those experiences which makes the traveller vow never to leave England again. However, the worst is over. We have just run through the Straits of Otranto, and are now under the lee of the Italian shore, expecting to arrive at Brindisi by 3 p.m., where I post this letter.

HOTEL DANIELI, VENICE,
Tuesday Morning, 13*th March*, 1877.

THE cold north wind, with a temperature just above freezing, has followed us all the way up the Adriatic, but fortunately, though cold and frosty, it was beautifully bright and clear yesterday morning as the "Avoca" approached Venice. I was on deck at 7 o'clock in the morning, and saw the bright Campaniles, and domes and towers of Venice rising out of the sea in the far distance, with the glorious background of the Styrian and Bavarian mountains stretching away from the east to west for nearly the half circle of the horizon, and all covered with snow. It was an unusually beautiful sight in the brilliant morning sun. We steamed up to Venice, and cast anchor in the Grand Canal, just opposite the Doge's Palace, at 10 o'clock yesterday morning, disembarked in a gondola, and obtained good rooms facing the canal at this hotel. Well, I can say nothing of this wonderful city, of the Piazza S. Marco, of the palaces and churches, of the great masterpiece of Titian, except what has been said before a thousand times. After gazing on the Titian I had no eye for any other picture in the gallery. I never was more struck with the power of côlour, or with the drawing of any picture I have ever seen. It is certainly an inspired work of the greatest colourist that ever lived. The Piazza S. Marco surpassed my expectations. Its beauty consists in its defiance of all the conventional laws of uniformity and of architecture. No group of buildings exist at all like it, nor can any be now built like it. It is absolutely perfect of its kind. We gondola'd about all yesterday; very cold it was—piercing cold—so as to spoil all one's pleasure; but I stick to Europe nevertheless, and am glad to be free from the heat, as well as from the dilapidation, ruin, débris, and crumbling away of the East. We leave this on Thursday morning for Milan; Saturday, Turin; and Monday, Paris.